Managing Corporate Reputation and Risk

Developing a Strategic Approach to Corporate Integrity Using Knowledge Management

Managing Corporate Reputation and Risk

Developing a Strategic Approach to Corporate Integrity Using Knowledge Management

DALE NEEF

ELSEVIER
BUTTERWORTH
HEINEMANN

Amsterdam   Boston   Heidelberg   London   New York   Oxford
Paris   San Diego   San Francisco   Singapore   Sydney   Tokyo

Butterworth–Heinemann is an imprint of Elsevier.

 Recognizing the importance of preserving what has been written, Elsevier Science prints its books on acid-free paper whenever possible.

Library of Congress Cataloging-in-Publication Data

Neef, Dale, 1959–
    Managing corporate reputation and risk / Dale Neef.
        p.   cm.
    Includes bibliographical references and index.
    ISBN 0-7506-7715-5
    1. Corporate image.   2. Corporations—Moral and ethical aspects.   3. Business ethics.
4. Integrity.   5. Risk management.   6. Knowledge management.   I. Title.

HD59.2.N44 2003
659.2–dc21

2003052325

British Library Cataloguing-in-Publication Data
A catalogue record for this book is available from the British Library.

The publisher offers special discounts on bulk orders of this book.
For information, please contact:

Manager of Special Sales
Elsevier Science
200 Wheeler Road
Burlington, MA 01803
Tel: 781-313-4700
Fax: 781-313-4882

For information on all Butterworth–Heinemann publications available, contact our World Wide Web home page at: http://www.bh.com

10 9 8 7 6 5 4 3 2 1

Printed in the United States of America

Table of Contents

Introduction

This book is about what a company needs to do to manage its integrity and to avoid making the kind of mistakes (an Environmental Protection Agency [EPA] fine, a product safety disaster, an employment lawsuit, an overseas worker exploitation charge) that can lead to penalties, a loss of share value, and a damaged corporate reputation.

Integrity in business has never been more important. In many ways, companies have a lot more to lose today than even 10 years ago, simply because the potential for being caught and exposed—by activists, lawyers, prosecutors, government agencies or the media—is greater than ever before. The penalties are larger—loss of share value, consumer boycotts, lawsuits, greater regulation—and more personal, with executives and board members increasingly being held accountable for the actions of the company with heavy personal fines and even imprisonment. The triple combination of personal-incentive–based pay, new levels of empowerment, and a leaner, more aggressive economy means that employees at all levels, as never before, are caught in that tug-of-war between doing what is right and doing what their superiors want and need, in order to achieve unrealistic targets. To avoid these types of disasters, companies need to do more than simply give money away in philanthropic gestures and claim that they are "socially responsible." They are going to have to start actively managing their risk in a much more effective way.

Putting aside some obvious cases of pure malfeasance on the part of corporate executives in recent scandals, the fact is that most reputation-damaging incidents happen because company decision makers, corporate officers, or board members simply don't know what is going on in their own organization. There are hundreds of good examples which demonstrate that if executives or senior managers had only known what was happening, they would have taken preventative action. The fact that they didn't know provides a compelling case for better knowledge management in the modern company.

What do companies need to do in order to avoid making costly and self-destructive mistakes? In this book, we look at the best-practice techniques that companies can use to protect their integrity and to avoid these costly blunders.

There are three important areas of focus. First, a company has to actively manage its process for ensuring corporate integrity. This means telling your employees that you expect—that is, require—ethical behavior and then putting together a better process for encouraging, monitoring, and enforcing that behavior by having employees at all levels of the company participate actively in anticipating and resolving ethical or legal issues. In short, companies need to establish a strong and effective ethical framework.

Second, a company has to actively gain a better understanding of what is happening both internal to the company and in the outside world so that it can sense potential problems and react to them in a responsive and ethical way. The good news is that never have we had so much knowledge and information at our fingertips or better techniques and systems to help us access, analyze, and act on that knowledge. This process is called *knowledge management*.

After all, whether it is a board not knowing that executives are completing off-the-books partnerships with company money or senior management having no idea that operational employees are dumping toxic wastes down local wells, these things are still essentially colossal failures of knowledge management. And as new punitive regulations from the U.S. sentencing guidelines agency and recent legislation such as the Sarbanes-Oxley act demonstrate, the excuse that "we didn't know" what was happening is no longer valid. Companies are today, more than ever before, expected—again, required—to know about and be responsible for the actions of their employees. Increasingly, a failure to manage company integrity can lead to severe penalties for the company and for executives themselves. In today's climate, "we didn't know" is no longer considered an excuse; it is considered to be negligence.

What is needed then is to apply many of the same knowledge management techniques and systems that have worked so successfully during the past 5 years in the operational world to a company-wide process for actively managing risk. It isn't that expensive, and it isn't even that difficult, but it doesn't just happen on its own; it's something that companies need to actively manage.

As the more progressive companies can demonstrate, applying these types of knowledge management techniques have many important benefits. Knowledge risk management (KRM) allows a company to anticipate issues, to avoid risks, and to behave more responsively and acceptably. It also applies many of the same tenets of quality management and can be used to improve processes, reduce waste and costs, and increase productivity. In short, using KRM to actively manage a company's integrity moves a company one step up the evolutionary ladder toward becoming both a more ethical and a more efficient organization.

Finally, not only is it important that companies actively manage their integrity, but it is also important that they can demonstrate to the outside world, including investors, activists, and consumers, that they are doing so. For this, a company needs to apply internationally recognized standards and to report their performance against those standards in a clear, accurate, and verifiable way. This can best be achieved using new triple–bottom-line reporting techniques that provide a broader and more accurate view of their organization's activities—financial, corporate governance, social, and environmental—for shareholders, analysts, pressure groups, and the media.

These three elements—developing a strong ethical framework, actively pursuing KRM, and reporting on those efforts using triple–bottom-line reporting techniques—are key to managing integrity in the modern corporation. It has never been more easily and efficiently done, and it has never been more important.

PART ONE

~

The Case
for Greater
Integrity

ONE

New Ethical Concerns for the Modern Corporation

A 16-month-old child dies from drinking bacteria-laden apple juice after a company ignores advice concerning the product's safety. A slaughterhouse is found dumping waste, chicken blood, and entrails into one of Mississippi's main water systems. A children's safety seat manufacturer fails to reveal to the public dangerous defects in its car seats, cribs, and strollers that kill two babies and injure more than 300 others. Enron collapses, costing employees millions of dollars in pension losses. Merrill Lynch agrees to pay $100 million in fines for touting stocks that its own analysts expected to lose money. Hundreds of listed companies are forced to restate their profits, caught red-handed in financial manipulation and deception.

Why do these things continue to happen? Just when economists, politicians, and business leaders were declaring the final triumph of free-market capitalism over central planning or government intervention in markets—just when the doctrine of corporate voluntary compliance was beginning to make headway against overregulation—it seems as if all the concerns and accusations levied by pressure groups against companies are justified.

Maybe it is because we were beginning to believe the constant upbeat advertising, the incessant almost orwellian re-branding, the slogans, the music, the pictures of happy children, pristine lakes, and dedicated employees that fill the airwaves, billboards, and the

Internet, thrown at us by corporate public relations campaigns. Facing activism from anti-capitalists, corporations over the past 2 years have clambered to raise their ethical profiles by presenting themselves— through philanthropy, community assistance, public relations programs, and advertisements—as caring and socially responsible companies.

We found ourselves suddenly disillusioned again, though, by a series of company scandals in 2001/2002, including those that led to the most devastating bankruptcies in corporate history. Of more concern, however, is that those executive-led accounting scandals are only the tip of the iceberg. Companies are continuing to do unethical and harmful things much as they always have, and they continue to be caught and fined in record amounts. There are many examples.

- In 2002 BP-Amoco pleaded guilty to a felony charge involving the illegal dumping of toxic waste at its Endicott oil field on the North Slope and was fined $22 million in civil and criminal penalties.
- According to a report by the Michigan Occupational Safety and Health Administration (MIOSHA) following a 7-month investigation, top Ford officials were well informed of the life-threatening hazards at their Dearborn, Michigan power plant before the explosion in 1999 that killed 6 workers and severely injured 14 others. According to MIOSHA, the reason, in part, that the study took so long to complete, was general obstruction in the investigation by Ford, including refusal to make safety records and other documents available. The report revealed that the gas explosion would not have occurred if Ford had installed a ventilation system that had been recommended by an internal Ford audit, by its insurance carrier, by an outside consulting firm, and by a joint Ford–United Auto Workers report. In September of that year, Ford agreed to pay $7 million in settlement.[1]

- Texaco, accused of race discrimination by six employees, agreed in 1997 to pay $115 million in settlement and $30 million more to improve the racial climate in the company. The story was carried in newspapers and on television worldwide and came on the back of a devastating recording of executives in a 1994 meeting, reported in the *New York Times*, using racial slurs against minority employees even as they discussed destroying documents linked to the lawsuit.[2]

The list of company disasters goes on and on: Enron, Tyco, Global Crossing, Coca-Cola, BP-Amoco, De Beers. . . . It is not only large multinationals, of course. Small and medium-sized companies continue to be found dumping toxic wastes, violating employment legislation, and creating and distributing unsafe products.

- Central Industries, a Mississippi poultry waste processor, was assessed some $14 million in fines and damages for dumping slaughterhouse waste—including feathers, entrails, and body parts—into a tributary of the Pearl River, part of Mississippi's central water supply.[3]
- DoubleClick, the Internet advertising business, was forced to suspend its policy of implanting electronic surveillance files—cookies—on Web surfers' hard drives without their knowledge. Accused of using information collected to compile and sell user profiles linked to e-mails (and therefore names and addresses), the company was forced to restrict its online profiling service through a settlement made after several states began legal action under the Consumer Protection Act. Not only is its brand name now synonymous with privacy violations on the Internet, but its share value has plummeted, it has been the subject of a Federal Trade Commission inquiry, has faced investigations by the states of Michigan and New York, and is involved in six related lawsuits.

- Cosco, the largest manufacturer of baby strollers and car seats in the United States agreed to pay $1.3 million as settlement after the Consumer Product Safety Commission (CPSC) charged the company with failure to inform the CPSC or the public of product defects with its cribs, strollers, car-seat carriers, and high chairs that caused the deaths of two babies and injured more than 300 children.[4]

The litany of callous, illegal, and unethical corporate behavior is breathtaking. Yet, none of these calamities came about because of natural disasters or unforeseeable events: They were man made and easily predictable. They came about either because company employees were purposely pursuing policies outside of boundaries of the public's ethical acceptance (*a failure of a company's ethical policy*), or almost worse, executives and board members did not know what policies their company was pursuing (*a failure of knowledge management*).

TRUTH OR CONSEQUENCES

As a result, of course, there has been a severe and predictable backlash. The combined effect of the 2001 scandals and the collapse in the dot-com market in the United States, Europe, and Japan has resulted in record bankruptcies, plunging share prices, and unprecedented penalties and fines for once well-known and trusted companies. New legislation in Europe, Canada, Australia, and Japan is set to ensure greater transparency and reporting on corporate governance, social, and environmental issues, requiring companies to begin demonstrating greater transparency by adding corporate governance, social, and environmental performance reviews to their annual reports.

In the United States, the Sarbanes-Oxley Act regulating financial service companies has been rushed into existence in the face of scandals, cobbled together with a frightening juxtaposition of all-encompassing rules and special exemptions. Chief executives now have to confirm by signature the validity of their financial reports, at risk of heavy personal fines and imprisonment if those figures, under audit, turn out to be invalid. Those accountancy groups that remain—after Andersen's ignominious collapse—have pledged to apply unprecedented rigor in future audits. And the public perception of the integrity of business advertising and business leaders is at record lows.

Further, as revelations of corporate wrongdoing have surfaced and the general outrage at corporate misbehavior has grown, penalties have become more stringent and more focused on personal, rather than corporate, responsibility. Each week brings footage of the newest "perp walk," with company executives, pale and bewildered, occasionally handcuffed, being escorted into court, with somber lawyers at their side. In the United States the Sentencing Guidelines Commission has made it clear that executives and board members who have not taken the appropriate precautions to guard against illegal or dangerous activities by their company can be held personally responsible—through fines and imprisonment—when these catastrophes do occur. Australia has just enacted a similar set of laws in its Commonwealth Criminal Code, and in 2000 Canada passed the Toughest Environmental Penalties Act, which includes a SWAT team to sweep down on businesses and allows fines for individual employees and executives of up to $4 million (Canadian) per day, with jail terms of up to 5 years.

At the same time, the Internet and CNN now provide a new and powerful communication medium for "business bashing," and a greatly expanded and voracious business press combine with powerful and effective nongovernmental organizations and pressure groups to provide unprecedented levels of scrutiny of company behavior. This makes companies vulnerable to almost instant repercussions for a corporate blunder. A corporate scandal can overwhelm a company in a matter of days, sullying reputations—Nike, Firestone, Enron, Tyco, Andersen—and leading to plunging share values. An incident involving child welfare, a product safety claim, or an Environmental Protection Agency (EPA) violation can quickly erode investor confidence, and if egregious enough, once publicized by pressure groups, can even lead to consumer boycotts, undermining the company's strategic flex-ibility, demoralizing the employees, and ultimately threatening the company's "license to operate." Punishment for bad behavior can be ruthless, particularly by shareholders, analysts, and banks.

Affected by a new level of global turmoil that began with 9/11, the global economy remains weak, promising to keep markets unstable for some time. Yet those markets—particularly Wall Street—remain focused on the all-important quarterly profits report. This continues to drive companies to take extraordinary measures—and risks—in order to maintain their share price in a never-ending struggle to main-tain the impression of high growth.

This weakened economy, of course, only compounds the relentless pressures that force companies to cut costs, find ways of generating ever greater efficiencies, and expand their reach into global markets. In fact, with the downturn in the global economy since 2000, the pres-sure to perform has increased, as companies continue to announce weak quarterly results and poor long-term forecasts. With fudging the numbers no longer an option, this has driven organizations to con-tinue to outsource, to expand their supplier base, or to relocate their manufacturing sites to developing countries, seeking lower labor costs and less regulation.

Of course, with the global extension of their supply chain, an orga-nization assumes a greater level of risk—from labor issues, corruption, or loose environmental standards—that can affect their overseas oper-ations, and once discovered, rock their operations at home. These sorts of incidents can suddenly make a good company seem callously indif-ferent and uncaring, with graphic pictures of poor working conditions or illegal chemical disposal being shown on the evening news in London, Toronto, or Chicago.

WHY GOOD COMPANIES DO BAD THINGS

Yet, companies still continue to commit egregious blunders on an almost daily basis. Why does this continue to happen? Why would a modern American company continue to dispose of illegal toxic wastes (or chicken carcasses) despoiling the environment, putting workers and the public at risk, with a very good chance of being caught and fined? Why do companies continue to ignore critical audits or internal warnings even though this may harm employees, the public, and ultimately their own company's reputation?

There have been many theories put forward about why good companies can do such bad things. One possible explanation lies in the new organizational and personal performance incentives that have been developed over the last decade and that have altered the traditional, more hierarchical, risk-averse and approval-focused organizational structures of the past. As the de-layering and downsizing continues, employees today have at once both greater freedom of action and more personal responsibility than ever before.

At the same time, personal incentive plans, ubiquitous now at every level of the organization, have made it possible for management to manipulate and focus employee performance, increasing productivity and efficiency. Working ever longer hours, a large component of the earnings of most salaried employees today are dependent upon achieving goals that reflect the ultimate concern of the company itself, that is, making the numbers each quarter.

These efficiency improvements, however, have not come without a price. As expectations for lifetime employment and single-company loyalty have faded, employees have become much more likely than ever before to sue their company or to take a workplace complaint into litigation. And with an increasing portion of their personal income dependent upon bonuses that are tied to high performance, the risk that employees will do whatever is necessary to achieve the desired results—cook the books, pay the bribe, or illegally dispose of waste materials—continues to grow. After all, despite their proclamations of being an ethical company and considerable contributions to worthy causes, Enron employees were under no illusion that if they did not make their quarterly numbers, they would lose a good portion of their earnings and face being summarily fired.

This feeling seems to be endemic to modern business. A recent survey by the Ethics Resource Center found that 43 percent of respondents believed that their supervisors didn't set good examples of integrity, and nearly the same number felt pressured to compromise their organization's ethics on the job.[5] When just less than one half of a country's employees are compromising their ethical standards under pressure from management, something is very wrong with our organizational culture.

In this type of culture, creativity and innovation soon became code words for illegal or unethical policies. It is a peculiar irony. We in business have become so skilled at encouraging people through personal gain to be productive for the company as a whole that we have turned a blind eye to the downside of this new attitude. Today, more than ever before, unethical or illegal behavior instituted by "creative" employees (such as those at Andersen, Tyco, Enron, or Barings) can mean the destruction of the corporation itself.

There have also been several fundamental changes to the organizational structures of the modern corporation in the past decade that have contributed to the likelihood of disasters. With global expansion of their supply chains, companies have inherited (usually unwillingly) extended responsibilities for the actions of third-party factories in developing countries, where their own reputation can be tarnished by local employment or environment violations. Fair or not, for example, for many people Nike is now synonymous with the term "sweat shop" because of its ruinous association with poor Southeast Asian factory practices. A single major incident can be disastrous to a company's reputation, and it takes a long time to regain that reputation through good works, or even, in Nike's case, diligent attempts at reform.

But We Didn't Know . . .

These are all contributory factors that may help to explain why companies continue to do things that are unethical and ultimately self-destructive. However, apart from the more general issue of new organizational structures and employee incentives, the most obvious reason why companies continue to commit reckless and illegal acts seems to be that *few organizations are really very good at knowledge and risk management (KRM).*

After all, most corporate disasters—a product safety violation, employing underaged workers, or illegal disposal of wastes—are not the sort of thing that company executives or board members would normally endorse. The reason most often cited when these disastrous incidents occur (these days, quite often in front of a judge) is that senior company leaders had no knowledge of what was taking place in their company. And, sadly, very often their claims of complete ignorance seem to be true.

What is surprising is that despite all the new pressures that companies face and the new organizational structures and incentives that tempt employees toward successful performance at any cost, little has been done to create a counterbalancing ethical climate in companies. As Stephen Albrecht, points out in his book, *Crisis Management for Corporate Self-Defense,* too often executives have little sense of the potential for a corporate disaster. "Those things happen at other companies," they respond. "We've never had that kind of problem here, so we don't waste time worrying about it."[6]

On the whole, even large and sophisticated companies seldom have a coordinated process for ensuring that ethical behavior exists. The ethics program is usually much the same as it has been for the past three decades: weak, administered by human resources only when a new employee joins the company, and focused on important but essentially nonoperational ethical issues (lying, cheating, or misusing company property).

The ubiquitous pastel-framed company value statement can be found in most corporate canteens, and yet no one takes the statement seriously or applies it to their day-to-day work. Boastful and challenging in tone, these statements are often focused more on inspiring employees to succeed in achieving their departmental targets than on any real concern for ethical behavior. "At Enron," says

Stuart Gilman, president of the Ethics Resource Center in Washington, D.C., "ethics was simply a piece of paper with three Ps—print, post [in the company lunch room], and then pray that something is actually going to happen."[7] If anything, these meager attempts simply undermine, through their very ineffectiveness, any real efforts to instill in employees an appreciation for the need for strong ethical behavior.

Nor have most companies tried to remedy the increased-risk situation structurally. Safety and environmental policies are administered on a compartmentalized basis and are seldom coordinated strategically. There are quality assurance and occupational health and safety groups, of course, but there are only tenuous links, in most companies, between experts in safety, legal, human resources, and operations. With little formal communication between these groups, companies almost never have a formal mechanism for early identification of a potential risk to the company's reputation, and when an incident does occur, companies seldom have a formal process for risk review, assessment, and resolution. It is not uncommon for failures, in safety, in compliance, or in environmental policies, to be covered up, with little fear of oversight or formal audits. It happens every day in businesses across the country and around the world, and the violations, fines, and product safety issues continue to mount.

In fact, most real decisions that can cause a company disaster are initially made at a first-level manager position, and only when things have gone very wrong do senior management, the chief executive, or board members get involved. And despite new legislation that requires board members to be actively engaged in the ethical and risk management process of the company, most board members of Fortune 500 companies have no practical role in operational risk management issues. Despite their own liability (for which insurance companies are increasingly charging ever higher premiums), most board members don't even know what risk management processes the company has in place. *This is surely one of the most compelling knowledge management issues ever raised.*

What companies have done, on the other hand, is to pour money into philanthropic and community causes under the co-opted label of "corporate social responsibility," hoping that giving out money will essentially buy goodwill among their stakeholders. This philanthropy, long a historical tradition in the United States, is a good thing in and of itself, but it has almost nothing to do with corporate social responsibility in any real sense. Beneficial to those receiving the money, of course, the fact remains that handing out community grants doesn't make a company behave better or prevent a catastrophe from occurring. And unfortunately, when a company boasts of being ethical and caring and yet is found to be in violation of financial regulations or social or environmental laws, they only increase the impression that much of the philanthropy and public displays of corporate social responsibility are nothing less than what has been termed "greenwash" by skeptical activists.

Make Ethics and Knowledge Management a Core Operational Competency

The good news is that even as demands for better behavior are pushing corporations toward reform, company executives have at their disposal a plethora of new tools, systems, incentives, and knowledge management practices that can help them to create a more ethical and risk-aware company culture. Organizations can use new information technology (IT)–based tools to enhance their profitability and to communicate easily and effectively to employees worldwide. Advances in supply chain and logistics practices and systems mean that companies have new global opportunities for ethical sourcing, manufacturing, and sales. The Internet and supporting IT technologies give company planners access to unprecedented high-quality information regarding competition, leading practices, scientific research, and new product announcements. Organizations can turn to accurate market analysis tools to understand potential market opportunities and risks and have instant access to journals, news wires, and complex and specialized business research and analysis systems. Safety and incident management applications can present senior management with accurate reports on safety violations, identifying trends that can reveal potentially damaging risks to come. In terms of new knowledge management techniques and information access, companies have never had it so good.

Moreover, most of these techniques, processes, and systems exist—or should exist—already in the modern company. Enterprise resource planning systems provide key company-wide performance data, and environmental health and safety systems exist that can record trends and provide early alert and incident management techniques. Knowledge management tools (e.g., e-mail, the Internet, early alert teams, communities of practice, and capturing and distributing "lessons learned") can all be applied in a formal process that will help a company to sense and respond to potential risks.

In fact, despite the increased risk to a corporation's reputation that comes with the new global environment, with all the advancements in IT, process, and management techniques made in the past two decades, companies have very little excuse for continuing to take a drubbing because of costly and predictable mistakes when it comes to corporate integrity issues. But all of this means rethinking the way that the organization approaches the issues of KRM, setting up an ethical framework as a company and reorganizing systems and processes specifically to focus on preventing ethical disasters.

PIONEERING COMPANIES

Some organizations, particularly those that are in the front line of potential problem areas such as apparel manufacturing, petroleum extraction, or chemicals, have made great strides in developing strong ethical programs and a coordinated approach to KRM. Many have been helped along by adopting the newly emerging standards for triple–bottom-line reporting, in which the company's social and environmental performance is openly measured and monitored. This is particularly true of European companies, with their close ties to national governments and a broad historical ethos of social responsibility.

What can we learn from these companies? What are the key aspects of their approach? There are four important areas of focus that leading companies incorporate into an integrated ethics and risk management program.

The first area of focus is to create *an ethical framework*. In many ways, this means building on many of the same techniques that have been a part of the corporate approach to ethics management over the years, such as value statements and code of conduct, but it also involves much more. One of the most important features of an updated ethics process is to establish the senior executive position of "chief risk and ethics officer," to take overall responsibility for helping to communicate the company's policies in these areas and for monitoring and enforcing adherence to a formal risk management process. There also needs to be much more active participation in the ethics and risk management process by the chief executive officer and board members, not only just for designing and endorsing the ethics and risk policies, but also for actively participating in risk assessments on an ongoing basis. Combined with a strong program of education and training for employees and suppliers, this ethical framework creates the foundation for conveying a company's values, setting forth guidelines for the standards of behavior and levels of risk awareness that are expected from all employees.

The second important area of focus for the modern corporation is to introduce a formal program of *enterprise-wide risk management*. This risk management process encourages employees at all levels of the organization to take on the responsibility for avoiding unethical or illegal behavior and for anticipating and alerting their managers to potential problems of noncompliance or danger. Combined with risk and incident management software, this process incorporates systems and techniques that help corporate leaders to monitor the organization much more effectively and to anticipate and quickly respond to potentially damaging issues.

Third, companies are applying *knowledge management* techniques that have been developed over the past few years to actively manage employee and stakeholder knowledge and experience in a way that contributes to risk prediction and response analysis. In fact, many experts would contend that risk management *is* knowledge management, in that it is only through the knowledge, experience, and skills of employees, shared collaboratively, that a company can anticipate and react to reputation-threatening risks. A number of systems and knowledge gathering and sharing techniques, when formalized, can provide the basis for a constant flow of prioritized information from those who know to those who need to know. As part of a formal program of risk and reputation management, knowledge management techniques can help to ensure that a company becomes aware of potential hot issues before they get out of control.

This is where knowledge management techniques and systems finally come into the mainstream of management processes, after struggling in many ways to find operational legitimacy for the past several years. For the first time, knowledge management is something more than a set of practices and systems that simply contributes to greater company efficiency. A program of integrated knowledge and risk management (KRM) is essential to good management of a modern organization. In short, "we didn't know" is no longer an acceptable defense. Not having the knowledge management systems in place becomes the equivalent of negligence.

The final area of focus is the application of *new international standards of conduct* for social, environmental, corporate governance, and product safety polices. Much like the International Organization for Standardization (ISO) quality and productivity standards that are a part of business today, these guidelines—SA 8000, ISO 14001, and many others—provide a consistent framework for monitoring and auditing performance in the organization. At the same time, when integrated well, the very process of applying these standards of conduct at an operational level not only helps to avoid potentially damaging incidents but also helps to turn early warnings of infringements into productivity improvements.

Adopting these standards for internal use is something that will be of value to any organization, but equally important, companies need to report their performance against these standards openly and honestly for the world to see. This "triple–bottom-line" (financial, environmental, and social) reporting provides the company and its various stakeholders with a much more balanced view of company performance, marking a shift away from a single focus on financial profit and loss accounting and moving toward a more comprehensive set of indicators in other areas of performance that indirectly affect the financial results, such as corporate governance, ethics, and social and environmental policy.

Publishing accurate and auditable reports on their performance against these international standards and having those reports audited—much as with current financial reports—by an independent third-party auditor is essential. Not only does this reporting process provide a structure for monitoring ethical operations within the company, but equally important, this type of reporting provides a useful way of demonstrating to the market your company's progressive policies. Good governance and risk management programs, fair social policies, and a concern for environmental sustainability all reflect a concern for long-term stability.

The combined application of these emerging performance standards and triple–bottom-line reporting can greatly change the focus of your company culture while both protecting and improving your corporate reputation. It is soon to be required by the European Union and Japan and is increasingly being demanded by analysts and investors as a way of judging the stability and managerial sophistication of companies in which they invest.

INTEGRATED KNOWLEDGE AND RISK MANAGEMENT: THE NEXT EVOLUTIONARY STEP FOR THE MODERN GLOBAL CORPORATION

Given the recent scandals and the multiplicity of pressures that coalesce under the umbrella of globalization, it is not surprising that a renewed emphasis on corporate social responsibility has reemerged so strongly in the past 3 years. This is not simply a reaction to the corruption and overexuberance of the late 1990s. The combined effects of globalization, corporate scandal, new laws, the Internet, landmark litigation, and the increasing primacy of business in our everyday lives are bringing about a much more fundamental and permanent shift in how corporations are expected to be governed and to behave. Not only are expectations for ethical behavior growing, but the repercussions for poor behavior are becoming more costly.

Although the corporate social responsibility movement has been alive for a number of years, buoyed primarily by environmental and human rights pressure groups, these new and separate pressures on corporations will fundamentally alter many of the management and organizational practices of the modern corporation and usher in a permanent shift toward greater legal and social expectations in the next 2 to 5 years. Integrated KRM, this new movement, brought on by needs of a rapidly changing global business climate and new demands for better behavior, is *one of the most important steps in the evolution of the modern corporation since business process reengineering a decade ago.*

In short, corporations are entering a new period in which they will be expected to behave in a much more socially responsible way than in the past and will need to be able to prove to a variety of stakeholders—regulators, litigants, pressure groups, customers, and shareholders—that they have in place strong and auditable programs for preventing social, governance, and environmental and product safety disasters. It is no longer a question of something that a company "should do" as portrayed by activists. Today it is increasingly a question of what a company "must do" as part of competing in the global marketplace.

CHAPTER ENDNOTES

[1] "CIS Reaches Historic Settlement Agreement with Ford and UAW," *Michigan Newswire*, September 2, 1999. Available from www.michigan.gov.

2 "The Texaco, Inc. $176.1 Million Settlement: New Precedent for Race Discrimination,"
   Web site for Cohen, Milstein, Hausfeld and Toll. Available from
   www.cmht.com/casewatch/cases/cwtexco3.htm.

3 Tammy Shaw, "Environmental Penalties Reach an All Time High," Sea Grant Law
   Center Web site. Available from www.olemiss.edu/orgs/masglp/high204.htm.

4 "Cosco, Safety 1st: Fined $1.75 Million for Failing to Report Product Defects,"
   Consumer Affairs, April 4, 2000; available from
   www.consumeraffairs.com/news/cosco.html.

5 Heesun Wee, "Corporate Ethics: Right Makes Might," *Businessweek*, April 11, 2002.
   Available from www.businessweek.com/bwdaily/dnflash/apr2002/nf20020411_6350.htm.

6 James Altfeld, "Review of, 'Crisis Management for Corporate Self-Defense' by Stephen,
   Albrecht" (AMACOM Books, New York, 2002). Available from
   www.bizsum.com/crisismanagement.htm.

7 Heesun Wee, "Corporate Ethics: Right Makes Might," *Businessweek*, April 11, 2002.
   Available from www.businessweek.com/bwdaily/dnflash/apr2002/nf20020411_6350.htm.

TWO

Making the Business Case for an Integrated Program of Ethics and Knowledge Management

So how do we begin to make the case that an organization these days needs to devote the same level of corporate leadership, operations, and systems on ethics and integrated knowledge and risk management as it does on quality or productivity programs? The case for action begins with a look at some of the revolutionary geopolitical, economic, and social changes that are changing the environment of the modern corporation.

Risks Associated with Global Reach

Globalization is one of the most emotional and least well-defined areas of modern debate. A phrase used to cover everything from trade relations to cultural clash, it is broadly associated with capitalism, inequality, exploitation, and western (and particularly American) multinationals. In fact, the concept has become so muddled with broader issues, such as fair trade, sustainability, and even the HIV/Aids pandemic, that it is difficult to pin down any boundaries to the debate.

Whatever else it means though, at the heart of the globalization debate lies the reality that western corporations are relocating their production and sales capacities internationally, particularly into developing economies, in order to take advantage of emerging consumer markets, a low-cost labor supply, lower tax regimes, and lower levels of environmental and employment oversight. Even if this trend has not occurred as suddenly or as uniquely as many activists would claim (most studies indicate that international trade has not increased that dramatically since the 19th century and days of imperialism, colonies, and empire), what is undeniably true is that the combination of opportunity and competition has driven companies during the last two decades to either relocate or to contract services from factories, call centers, and sales offices throughout the developing world.

In fact, almost every major U.S. or European corporation is now, and has been for at least a decade, involved in an expansion of their production and sales functions to overseas markets. A company such as DHL, the parcel delivery service, for example, now operates in 229 countries and territories. Some 40 percent of General Electric's revenue comes from overseas operations. Intel has 80,000 employees in offices sprinkled around 40 countries. Apparel and footwear companies such as Nike, Gap, or Reebok contract production through a network of hundreds of different third-party factories, mostly located in these developing markets. These companies may have only a few thousand direct employees but may engage several hundred thousand workers indirectly through these third-party relationships.

This global expansion has forced companies to change the way they perceive competition and growth and has required fundamental changes to organizational structures, systems, and business processes. But above all, it has forced companies to deal with issues that are sometimes very different from those they encounter in their own domestic markets (e.g., risks such as corruption, sweat shops, employing children, or nonexistent environmental policies) for which they are increasingly being held to account by a strong and vocal movement that has arisen from international organizations, nongovernmental organizations (NGOs), pressure groups, unions, shareholders, and the informed public. Supported by an increasingly open international press, these "stakeholders" are demanding that corporations adhere to higher ethical standards with regard to governance, reporting, employment, and the environment.

In fact, much of the reason for the backlash against corporate relocation into these markets comes from a legitimate concern that, unchecked, the size and influence of the modern company would give it the power to overwhelm the undeveloped world, taking advantage of local employment and resources without regard to human rights, the environment, or the future of those communities. And unfortunately, far too many incidents have proven these fears to be well founded.

- Royal Dutch/Shell faced an international outcry when Saro-Wiwa, a Nigerian environmentalist, and eight other activists in Nigeria were hanged for what appeared to be their political opposition to Shell's local activities. Coming on the back of the Brent Spar oil platform controversy and amid consumer boycotts of Shell stations and an insistence by Shell shareholders that there was a difference "between noninterference and abrogation of responsibility," the value of Shell's brand name and its share price plummeted. In 2002 Royal Dutch/Shell was fined $40 million to pay for an oil spill in the region, and a U.S. court has ruled that the Royal Dutch Petroleum Company can be held liable in the United States for cooperating in the persecution and execution of the environmental activists in Nigeria. The whole affair was a public relations shambles and a shareholders' nightmare.

- When international human rights groups revealed that Nike supplier factories in Vietnam and Indonesia were employing workers, sometimes children, at wages as low as 20 cents an hour for up to 14 hours a day, Nike's brand name quickly became associated with sweat shops and third-world worker exploitation. Under criticism from human rights activists, as well as the *Wall Street Journal,* CBS News, and the *New York*

Times, Nike has come under almost constant scrutiny for its overseas manufacturing practices, initially reducing worldwide sales and requiring it to fund an ongoing and expensive public relations campaign.

Obviously, not all multinationals are guilty of these types of incidents, but the reality is that with relocation to a developing market comes fundamental new problems in terms of corporate governance and social and environmental behavior. The arguments for and against globalization are complex and important, but whatever your particular position as a corporation, it is important to realize that these and similar issues mean that your company will probably be facing a challenging future in terms of developing formal social and environmental policies for those overseas operations. Ultimately, the way a company behaves in these areas is much more important than donations to local charities and a Web site boasting of good corporate citizenship through philanthropy. In short, whatever your position on globalization, the effect on your company, even companies not directly involved in global affairs, is likely to be a greater need for an ethical framework, transparency, and nonfinancial reporting.

THE NEW INFORMATION SOCIETY

As companies and cultures are becoming more globalized, the combination of the Internet and new satellite and cable television technologies has made the distribution of information—instantly from virtually anywhere in the world—a part of our day-to-day lives. The Internet has particularly become a medium for quickly and effectively relaying information around the world.

Nowhere has the use of these new communication technologies been put to greater effect than by pressure groups in their prompt and dramatic exposure of corporate offenses. A quick search for "corporate social responsibility" (CSR) over the Web demonstrates how very effective the Internet has become in this regard. With hundreds of Web pages, chat sites, and discussion groups active on various social and environmental issues, companies are named and shamed.

"Each day," Kalle Lasn, editor of *Adbusters* magazine, candidly explains, "information about Nike flows freely via e-mail between the U.S. National Labour Committee and Campaign for Labour Rights; the Dutch-based Clean Clothes Campaign; the Australian Fairwear Campaign; and many others spread throughout the world."[1]

From the Brazilian rain forests to Nigeria, and from the diamond mines of South Africa to the oil fields in Alaska, company activities are mercilessly monitored by an increasingly powerful and effective cadre of activists who quickly relay information worldwide, into collaborative activist networks, to lobbyists, to government agencies, and to the press.

"Given developments in the electronic media and the Internet," affirms Dr. Brendan O'Dwyer at Dublin City University Business School, "these companies claim they now operate in a 'goldfish bowl' environment or 'CNN world' where no organization is able to shield its activities from the public gaze and from criticism in the wider society."[2]

This ability to name and shame companies, suddenly and forcefully brought about through the Internet and global television coverage, provides companies with a powerful incentive to protect their reputation through better behavior.

Pressure Group Activism

One of the most important new pressures for better business behavior to emerge in the past decade, of course, comes from the increasingly powerful and effective collection of pressure groups that monitor corporate behavior. NGOs such as Greenpeace, Oxfam, Amnesty International, CorpWatch, and the World Wildlife Fund (to name only a few) are increasingly able to uncover things on a new and unprecedented scale—poor employment policies, unethical investments, and environmental exploitation—that companies expected to be able to keep hidden from public view only a decade ago.

Better financed and managed than in the past, these professional pressure groups have been able to attract capable and dedicated employees who can match wits and tactics with a corporation's public relations or legal machine. Once perceived by many as extreme, in light of continued bad behavior by companies, these groups today are widely respected for their efforts. In Europe, for example, NGOs generally are now rated by the public as more highly regarded than leading businesses by a margin of nearly two to one. In a recent study conducted by Edelman Public Relations Worldwide, Amnesty International, the World Wildlife Fund, and Greenpeace scored between 62 and 76 percent on "trust" among the public, where even the most highly regarded companies (e.g., Microsoft, Bayer, Shell, and Ford) ranked only between 35 and 46 percent.[3] Nike provides a good example of the phenomenon.

"In a September 1997 press release," explains John Samuel, from InfoChange, "Nike dismissed its critics as 'fringe groups.' But by March 1998 it was ready to treat Nike's online critics with more respect. It introduced yet another package of labour reforms and admitted, 'You make changes because it's the right thing to do. But obviously our actions have been accelerated because of the World Wide Web.'"[4]

IdealsWork.com is another good example of how pressure groups are forcing companies toward better behavior. An online shopping site, IdealsWork.com provides information on the CSR performance of companies so that consumers can review a company's behavior before buying its product.

"Until now, information on companies' social and environmental records has only been available to the investment community, and has been used primarily by socially responsible investors," explains Dan Porter, co-CEO. "IdealsWork.com has made this information conveniently available to consumers for the first time. Now, through our partnership with UFE (United for a Fair Economy), we are providing important additional information on corporate accountability that we think consumers want in the aftermath of Enron and recent corporate scandals."5

The site rates companies based on their performance in such areas as labor practices, human rights, diversity, and the environment, and it has created a "Top 100 Worst" list for corporate offenders, listing companies that have committed unethical ("Enronesque" in their terms) behavior including high levels of political campaign contributions and lobbying expenditures, corporate tax avoidance, requirements for in-company 401K plan investments by employees, and combined consulting and auditing work being contracted from the same accounting group.6

It is just this type of thing that makes company executives nervous. And rightly so, points out Rob Harrison, co-editor of *Ethical Consumer*. The thing every company fears most is becoming the target of these powerful pressure groups or making one of the "Top Ten Worst" lists.

"So, rather than wait for it to happen," he explains, "managers are taking preemptive action in the form of environmental product development and labeling, or engaging in such ideas as codes of conduct and social audits."7

The Increased Power of Investors and Shareholders

The rise of the Internet has had other unexpected consequences on the modern corporation. As it has become possible to monitor and trade stocks in "real time" over the Internet, share ownership has expanded enormously, providing the opportunity for millions of citizens to buy and sell shares from their homes. With institutional and individual investments combined, more than 100 million Americans now own shares. This means that company ownership is now spread among nearly one third of the population, with most of these investors having a keen and newly discovered interest in a company's behavior. The United States is not alone, of course. During the past decade, financial markets have expanded throughout Europe and Asia. Fifty percent of Australian adults (7.3 million people) own shares in their own name or through a managed fund.[8] In Sweden, nearly 80 percent of adults own stock, the highest rate of public share ownership in the world.

With this level of popular management and ownership of shares, it seems intuitive that companies will have become much more susceptible than ever before to incidents that might damage their reputation and send their share value plummeting. Well-publicized cases demonstrate what scandal can do to a share price. Martha Stewart's Living Omnimedia lost 21 percent in the first 5 days in June 2002 when she first faced allegations of insider trading with ImClone. Electronic Data System's stock fell 10 percent in 1 day on news of a Securities and Exchange Commission (SEC) probe. When HealthSouth restated its earnings in August 2002, the company's shares fell 44 percent in 1 day. When news broke of an SEC investigation for insider trading, the company's shares plunged a further 27 percent.[9] In fact, a recent study from the University of Southwestern Louisiana estimated that unethical corporate behavior lowers stock prices for a minimum of 6 months.[10]

Often only marginally informed about the companies in which they own shares, individual traders are particularly susceptible to negative reports about companies that appear in the press. They are easily swayed by the opinions of popular analysts or by reports of mismanagement or executive scandal, and the announcement of litigation or an environmental or employment violation reported on the evening news can mean an after-dinner rush to the computer to sell, sending share prices spiraling downward the next morning. Even if they have no genuine concern about the morality or rightful responsibility of the incident itself, everyone knows that scandal will harm the share value. Even institutional investors are drawn into the panic, aware that whatever the inherent value of the stock, negative reports tend to create a run on company shares.

There is another important aspect to this popular investment phenomenon. The combination of poor governance, inaccurate financial reporting, and the collapse of the dot-com bubble has meant that billions of dollars have been lost by investors during the past few years, the sort of thing that makes investors crave accurate, verifiable information from companies. Accordingly, investors (particularly institutional investors) want to know about the quality of a company's management team, its approach to corporate governance, and increasingly, the company's position on volatile issues such as employment conditions in developing world sites or environmental policies in developing countries. The more institutional investors can learn dependably from a company's reporting process, the more likely they are to be willing to invest in company shares. A recent Harris Interactive poll, for example, found that 71 percent of Americans claim to consider corporate citizenship issues when they make investment decisions.[11]

But such is the mistrust of companies by the investment community following the 2002 scandals, that this type of information is useful (and believable) only if it is based on internationally approved comparable standards, verified in turn by independent and credible third-party auditors. That is why a company that adopts a formal ethics and KRM process and applies independently verified triple–bottom-line reporting standards stands out as progressive and transparent (the very attributes that investors like to see in a company).

LEGISLATION AND LITIGATION

In Europe, where companies are expected to share a greater social burden, the CSR movement has taken on a powerful momentum and is now rapidly becoming enshrined not only at the corporate level but also in country and European Union (EU) law.

The European Commission has been particularly active in promoting greater corporate social responsibility, stating openly in a recent communiqué that "as there is evidence suggesting that CSR creates value for society by contributing to a more sustainable development, there is a role for public authorities in promoting socially and environmentally responsible practices by enterprises."[12] The commission is also debating the idea of setting up a European ombudsman to help adjudicate over CSR-related issues that arise from the overseas operations of European companies. The European Parliament recently approved a supporting resolution, requiring companies to supply information concerning their social and environmental policies while setting aside funds for promoting CSR policies and training initiatives among European companies.

At the national level, too, European governments have been strongly supportive of greater social and environmental accountability by companies. Britain, for example, has established an office for CSR at the cabinet level, for which the trade and industry secretary is responsible. The United Kingdom has been focused on issues of corporate governance and risk management since the Cadbury report, commissioned by the government in 1992. More recently, the Turnbull report in 1999, also commissioned by the government, was partly responsible for important corporate governance changes such as the separation of the roles of chief executive officer and chairman. Aligning itself with groups such as the International Labor Organization and the Organization for Economic Cooperation and Development's (OECD) work with multinational enterprises, the U.K. government also announced in 2002 its support for the creation of new guidelines for CSR management and reporting in the financial services sector, with the view to providing assistance to financial services organizations in auditing social and environmental reports. Very much at the center of the CSR movement, the United Kingdom has a highly developed group of CSR consultancies, initiatives, and advocates from NGOs, government, and business. In SustainAbility's recent "Top 50 Sustainability Companies," the top seven companies were all British.

This Anglo-European drive toward CSR and triple–bottom-line reporting is beginning to bring pressure on U.S. companies as well.

As Jim Kartalia, president of Entegra Corporation points out, "Any American corporation that wants to do business globally is going to be forced to address these issues. The EU is pushing this legislation and they are going to force American companies to comply or else they are not going to get business."[13]

France has taken an even more progressive posture, passing legislation in February 2002 that would make it mandatory for all companies listed on the "premier marché" (those with the largest market capitalization) to account for their environmental and social performance in their annual reports from 2003. Reporting requirements would include sustainability information, such as a company's consumption of water and energy, energy emissions, and biodiversity efforts, as well as a description of their programs to reduce environmental risks and to educate employees on leading practices in environmental management. Companies are also required to provide performance information on their activities in the areas of human resources and community and labor standards.[14] It is an interesting idea. The law doesn't require any specific activity or performance standard of a company; it merely requires a company to transparently report on its efforts in these areas. The idea is that the competition that comes with transparency will create the incentive.

Even European business schools are strongly endorsing an effort to revolutionize business education, integrating CSR theories and leading practices into their core MBA curriculum. Skeptical of the value of the established shareholder value model, they are determined to instill in future business managers of European corporations a broader sense of devotion to stakeholders, to sustainability, and to society as a whole.

In the United States, nonfinancial reporting is likely to remain voluntary for the foreseeable future, but with recent scandals, other types of legislation have been proposed or passed. At the federal level, of course, Sarbanes-Oxley, covering corporate governance and the securities industry, is probably the best known. Probably more important, as recent corporate indictments concerning financial irregularities have shown, U.S. Sentencing Commission guidelines mean stiff penalties for companies that are found guilty of violations and can't demonstrate that they have made a legitimate effort to curb unethical behavior in their organization or extended supply chain.

Prompted by a directive in Sarbanes-Oxley, many of the commission's guidelines have been made even more severe, accompanied with restrictions giving judges little flexibility in departing from those guidelines. As of January 2003, when a company officer is found guilty of defrauding more than 250 employees out of $1 million or more, the normal sentencing guidelines will be virtually doubled (like speeding in a construction zone), leaving the executive to face a minimum of 10 years in prison. Employees convicted of shredding documents in an attempt to obstruct justice will face 3 years in prison, and executives who sign corporate financial reports knowing that they are not in compliance with SEC rules can now be sentenced to 10 years in prison. It is a frightening and compelling case for better ethics and knowledge management.[15]

There is no lack of recent evidence to demonstrate that blunders can be costly—even ruinous—to companies. The criminal prosecution and conviction of Andersen, fined only $500,000 for obstruction of justice, essentially destroyed the company. ConAgra, recently paid $8.3 million for wire fraud, and Archer Daniels Midland was fined $100 million for price fixing. Following numerous Food and Drug Administration (FDA) inspections of its New Jersey and Puerto Rican production facilities, Schering Plough announced that it would pay a staggering $500 million to settle charges of repeated safety violations and failure over the years to correct manufacturing, quality assurance, laboratory, and packaging and labeling problems. That sort of money makes funding an effective ethics and knowledge management process seem a very good return on investment.

Attempts to hold companies responsible in U.S. civil courts for activities committed by those corporations overseas have also seen recent success. The Alien Tort Claims Act, now being leveraged in several court cases, will potentially allow claimants to sue U.S.

companies in the United States for human rights abuses or for complicity with groups or governments overseas engaged in these types of abuse, moving litigation forcefully into the international arena. A U.S. federal court, for example, ruled in March of 2002 that Shell Oil, in the long-running *Wiwa v. Royal Dutch Petroleum Co.* case concerning human rights violations in Nigeria, could (if convicted) be held liable in U.S. courts for abetting Nigerian security services in the persecution and execution of environmental activists in Nigeria.

Although in the past, these types of lawsuits were traditionally civil actions brought by individuals or through class action suits, recently many of the most damaging indictments for inappropriate corporate behavior have been brought as criminal actions against companies or company executives by state attorneys general. Elliot Spitzer, the attorney general for New York, is one of the most active in this area. Responsible for bringing indictments against many of the corporate executives during the millennium scandals, Spitzer also leveraged New York's Martin Act to demand a $100 million settlement from Merrill Lynch for impropriety by its analysts and investment banking group when it was revealed through company e-mails that company analysts were publicly endorsing stocks that they privately referred to as "junk" and worse. Similarly, the recent class action suit against Smith & Wesson gun manufacturers was brought, in part, by Richard Blumenthal, the attorney general of Connecticut. Taking advantage of newly confirmed constitutional powers, the states themselves have begun to hold companies to account as never before.

Equally important, liability has been shifting recently from the corporate to the personal, with executives and board members increasingly being named in corporate lawsuits. Senior executives are routinely held responsible for the illegal activities of employees (see Chapter 3), and increasingly, the courts are extending blame into the ranks of the boardroom.

"One of the biggest risks facing today's board members is being named in a corporate lawsuit," says John Nash, former president of the National Association of Corporate Directors. "Generally, directors have long been protected from being responsible for the actions of the corporate managers. But those times have changed."

"We are seeing the incidences of lawsuits filed against corporate directors increase 10% per year," Nash says. "Along with the potential to tarnish the individual's reputation, these lawsuits bring with them the stark reality of multi–million dollar fines and prison terms. And while a company may pay a fine for a director, it cannot go to prison for him or her."[16]

MAKING A POSITIVE BUSINESS CASE FOR RISK MANAGEMENT AND ETHICS

This combination of public and NGO pressure, shareholder demands, new legislation, and more successful litigation means new levels of accountability for companies, executives, and board members. Add to these pressures higher fines and the risk of personal penalties or imprisonment, and there is a compelling case for action for companies to initiate effective ethics and KRM programs.

However, the "business case" for an integrated ethical KRM framework is not all negative. Progressive companies that have initiated an integrated framework have found that there are many positive benefits that come from this type of approach as well.

Enhanced Brand Image, Improved Share Value, Increased Sales and Customer Loyalty

As we will see later in this book, one of the easiest ways to increase a company's brand value—with all the sales and share value benefits that come from that—is to be able to demonstrate openly and credibly that the company has a strong ethical framework and has adopted progressive social and environmental policies. "Reputation," says Ronald Alsop, author of *The Best Corporate Reputations in America,* "is much more than an abstract concept: It is a corporate asset that is a magnet to attract customers, employees, and investors."

Attracting and Retaining Employees

Good employees want to belong to a good company, and as the popularity of "Top 100 Best Company Lists" among job seekers demonstrates, corporate reputation is an important factor in a potential employee's decision to join, and for good employees to remain. So strong is that desire to be proud of the company for which they work, that a study by Net Impact of 2100 MBA students found that more than half of the students said they would accept a lower salary in order to work for a socially responsible company.[17]

As an executive from a prominent British petroleum company pointed out at a recent seminar, "People would be surprised at how many members of Greenpeace and the World Wildlife Fund there are in our organization—we want to be proud of our company and our environmental policies too."

Matching Improvements in Integrity with Efficiency Improvements

Combining an ethical framework with improved risk management techniques tends to uncover a multitude of issues concerning safety, productivity, and quality that would otherwise remain undetected. Effectively applied, an integrated KRM process can be used to extract relevant information from environmental health and safety systems, helping a company to remove "faults" in operational processes in much the same way as a quality or productivity assurance program. Many companies, from Chiquita to Intel, have found that applying these types of programs not only helps a company to avoid potential reputation-damaging incidents, but also helps to improve operational efficiency.

A recent collaborative study of 176 companies in 60 countries completed by SustainAbility and the World Bank's International Finance Corporation found that "sustainability" practices that lead to improvements in areas such as corporate governance, the environment, or health and safety policies had a multitude of other benefits, including lower costs, reduced risk, higher staff morale, and improved access to capital.[18]

British Telecom, an organization at the forefront of combining progressive ethical, environmental, and social policies to the workplace, insists that it can demonstrate a clear correlation between its reputation for good behavior and customer satisfaction. The company maintains that at least 25 percent of its good reputation is attributable to its efforts in these areas, and that if it were to subsequently lose that reputation—by abandoning these types of activities or by experiencing a reputation-damaging incident—that it would expect a 10 percent drop in customer satisfaction, and thus a similar drop in sales and profit.[19]

Reduced Regulatory Oversight

Corporations that can demonstrate that they have in place ethical, health and safety, environmental, and risk management processes that go beyond minimum regulatory compliance requirements will find that they receive much less scrutiny by regulatory agencies than companies that don't have these types of mechanisms in place. This can mean quicker approvals for permits, fewer inspections, and much greater strategic flexibility. Moreover, the goodwill that a company gains from taking proactive measures will go a long way if things go wrong.

A Competitive Edge

Finally, companies that put in place a broad program of ethics, international standards, and risk management tend to be more successful. Whether because of goodwill, strategic agility, attracting and retaining better employees, or higher levels of productivity, companies that have put these types of programs in place tend to gain an overall competitive edge. As Harold Kahn, leader of PricewaterhouseCoopers' U.S. Reputation Assurance practice says, "Our experience indicates that companies that actively manage these issues are most likely to be accepted in emerging markets, successfully launch new products, and recover from sudden and unexpected events such as product recalls and other possible reputation crises."[20]

Rapid Uptake

This movement toward greater corporate responsibility has been given a new impetus by recent corporate scandals, and is in many ways similar to the environmental movement in the mid-1990s that produced stronger regulations and gave rise to new international standards and Environmental Management Systems. "It is almost a carbon copy of what happened in terms of environmental issues six or seven years ago," explains Hewitt Roberts, chief executive of Entropy International. "In 1996 there had been a number of very significant events that happened at more or less the same time—the rise of the international standard, the Exxon Valdez, Chernobyl, Bopal, and Brent Spar—all coming to the fore at the same time as a consumer-led movement that pushed environmental issues up the corporate ladder."

"What is happening now," he concludes, "is the same thing except it is a wider issue, it is moving faster, and there is a greater degree of consensus. It is hitting the corporate agenda harder and higher."[21]

John Browne, director of Reputation Assurance at PricewaterhouseCoopers, agrees, concluding that for the next 50 years, "successful companies will be those who embed social, environmental, and ethical risk management into their core business processes and performance measures."

"This integrated approach," he concludes, "is at the heart of managing the 21st century company's most valuable asset—its reputation."[22]

Chapter Endnotes

[1] John Samuel, "Perspectives on Corporate Social Responsibility." Available from www.infochangeindia.org/corporatesrlbp.jsp.

2 Brendan O'Dwyer, "Social & Ethical Accounting, Auditing and Reporting," *Accountancy Ireland,* December 2000. Available from www.icai.ie/accountancy-ireland/articles/seaar.htm.

3 "U.S. Attitudes on CSR Move Closer to Europe's," *Holmes Report,* April 25, 2002. Available from www.holmesreport.com.

4 John Samuel, "Background and Perspective," InfoChange. Available from www.infochangeindia.org/corporatesribp.jsp; and David Segal and Caroline E. Mayer "Sites for Sore Consumers," *Washington Post,* March 29, 1999.

5 "Identifying Corporate Offenders," Tomorrow Publishing, August 21, 2002. Available from www.tomorrow-web.com/2002/aug/020821.html.

6 "Identifying Corporate Offenders," Tomorrow Publishing, August 21, 2002. Available from www.tomorrow-web.com/2002/aug/020821.html.

7 Rob Harrison, "Consumers Can Make All the Difference," InfoChange, 2000 [as cited by John Samuel in "Background and Perspective"]. Available from www.infochangeindia.org/corporatesribp.jsp.

8 "ASX and Share Ownership," Australia Coop Web site, February 6, 2003. Available from www.australia.coop/asx_share_own.htm.

9 Adrian Michaels, "Diagnosis of Fraud," *The Financial Times,* April 15, 2003.

10 "Human Rights," Business for Social Responsibility Web Site, May 2, 2002. Available from www.bsr.org.

11 "Consumers Skeptical of Corporate Citizenship Activities," *Holmes Report,* April 25, 2002, p. 1. Available from www.holmesreport.com.

12 Tim Dickson, "The Financial Case for Behaving Responsibility," *Financial Times,* August 19, 2002, p. 5.

13 Jim Kartalia, telephone interview with the author, January 23, 2002.

14 For a detailed explanation and critique, visit the Social Accountability Web site (www.sa-intl.org).

15 Carrie Johnson, "Panel Boosts Penalties for White-Collar Offenses," *Washington Post,* January 9, 2003 p. E01.

16 Victoria Wesseler, "Corporate Board Membership: Risky Business," Ethics and Compliance Strategies Web site. Available from www.ethicscompliance.com/main/marticles.html.

17 "Human Rights," Business for Social Responsibility Web site, May 2, 2002. Available from www.bsr.org.

18 Alison Maitland, "Developing Nations Win by Getting Greener," *Financial Times,* June 27, 2002.

[19] Tim Dickson, "The Financial Case for Behaving Responsibility," *Financial Times,* August 19, 2002, p. 5.

[20] "Surveys Find Many Consumers Hold Companies Responsible for Their Actions," from Press Room on the PricewaterhouseCoopers Web site, September 30, 1999. Available from www.pwcglobal.com.

[21] Hewitt Roberts, interviewed by the author, February 19, 2003.

[22] Brendan O'Dwyer, "Social & Ethical Accounting, Auditing and Reporting," *Accountancy Ireland,* December 2000. Available from www.icai.ie/accountancy-ireland/articles/seaar.htm.

THREE

Key Areas of Risk: Where Knowing What is Happening Really Matters

Managing a modern corporation today presents significant new challenges well beyond what was imagined just a decade ago. If your organization is involved with overseas sourcing, sales, or production, you're already aware of the myriad operational risks that face the modern multinational. But unstable regimes, bribery, and local corruption—long a source of concern—are only a part of that challenge. As we saw in Chapter 2, increasingly, NGOs, the press, and local pressure groups are demanding that companies refrain from practices (that they pursue themselves or that are done in their name through their subcontractors) that violate employment and human rights standards or threaten the environment along a supply chain (extended responsibility chain) that can extend around the world.

What is more, it is wrong to believe that ethical failures and significant risk are limited to foreign markets. As we have seen with recent corporate scandals, there are a multitude of examples in which poor governance reviews, haphazard workforce policies, or negligent environmental practices have incurred enormous financial and reputational penalties to companies functioning entirely in the United States, Canada, Europe, Australia, or Japan. The risk in terms of financial penalty and further litigation over domestic incidents is, on average, much greater than the risk for incidents that occur overseas.

Genetically modified foods, bioethics, political contributions, corruption and bribery policies, animal welfare—the list of potential issues facing the modern corporation is endless, and each of these risk areas, of course, must be analyzed on its own merit and in the context of your business framework. For the sake of simplicity though, it is possible to break down likely threats to the modern corporation into four broad categories:

- Corporate governance
- Environmental policies
- Employment and human rights
- Product safety

CORPORATE ACCOUNTABILITY AND GOVERNANCE

In the midst of the scandals concerning executive-sponsored accounting fraud and general corporate mismanagement, it is important to remember that until Enron's collapse, most of the ethical incidents that plagued companies—costing them share value, financial penalties, or customer loyalty—came not from problems with corporate governance, but with issues concerning product safety or violations of employment or environmental laws.

In fact, until the 2001/2002 spate of corporate accounting scandals surfaced, corporate governance would not have normally been thought of in the context of a book concerned with crises detection and risk management. It was always assumed in the past (now, we realize, wrongly) that company executives were the ones most concerned with the welfare of the company and therefore would be the ones attempting to monitor wrongdoing—not the ones being monitored.

This is not always the case, obviously, and given the catastrophic losses to shareholders and employees with recent scandals, it is impossible to cover the topic of how to use knowledge and risk management (KRM) techniques to avoid ethical disasters and not devote some time to the topic of corporate governance. As we have seen, executive misconduct and board indifference or ignorance can ruin a company as fast as an oil spill or a child employment scandal. In short, the failure of corporate governance is not only an ethical issue, but also a risk management issue.

Recent board and executive malfeasance scandals certainly meet the criteria for a corporate ethical management crisis. First, these scandals have almost universally involved serious unethical activities by employees (albeit often senior executive employees) that have threatened the livelihood and reputation of the firm. Second, these crises (at least if the other organizational leaders of the companies are to be believed) have also been largely due to a lack of knowledge about what employees were doing and how seemingly acceptable strategic policies might have a ruinous outcome. Finally, they have almost always involved a serious breach in accurate reporting and transparency.

It was hard not to feel incredulous when hearing Kenneth Lay and Jeffrey Skilling, after swearing under oath to a Senate subcommittee, explain that in defense of their actions at Enron, neither they nor their board actually knew what was taking place in their own company.

And of course Enron was only one of the many scandals to plague the U.S. corporate world. Dennis Kozlowski, CEO of Tyco, was indicted on charges that he evaded more than $1 million in taxes. His CFO, Mark Swartz, was charged in Manhattan with stealing $170 million. WorldCom became America's largest corporate bankruptcy in history in July 2002 after disclosing a $3.8 billion accounting fraud and firing its CFO, Scott Sullivan. Global Crossing, Adelphia, ImClone, HealthSouth—the list goes on and on.

The effect of this alleged executive-led fraud has affected the business landscape in several important ways. Aside from ruining the companies themselves, these bankruptcies have caused untold grief with displacement, and more seriously, the loss of employee pension funds. The numbers are staggering: California's state pension fund lost approximately $565 million on the collapse of WorldCom alone. New York State's pension fund lost nearly $300 million; Michigan $116 million; and Florida more than $85 million. The American Federation of State, County, and Municipal Employees (AFSCME) estimates that its members lost $1.5 billion worth of pension money with the collapse of Enron.[1]

The scandals have also significantly undermined, for many people, the concept of "shareholder value," in that by providing executives and boards with a single all-important target—share value—company leaders, abetted by banks and the accountancy industry, continually made the necessary accounting adjustments (whatever the underlying business reality) in order to keep that share price at record highs. It was no coincidence that executive salaries and bonuses were tied directly to the value of that share price. Not only were their self-enriching policies misleading and oftentimes illegal, but they encouraged hiding the massive amounts of debt that were accumulating like a time bomb for employees and the company as a whole.

Naturally, these scandals have had a large effect on the economy more broadly. An outrageous misallocation of capital, these policies meant that nonexistent money was being used to fuel the stock market bubble. And as the world has become used to seeing once highly respected corporate executives being led to and from court in handcuffs, the business community has suffered badly from a trust deficit, just at a time when confidence was what was needed most. An investigation by the *Financial Times* revealed that top executives—derisively named by the *Financial Times* as the "barons of bankruptcy"—had extracted some $3.3 billion from companies in personal remuneration even as they were driving them into bankruptcy.[2]

The cost to economic growth has also been significant. According to a recent Brookings Institute study, the affect of recent corporate scandals will probably cost the U.S. economy a staggering $35 billion; estimates range between 1 and 2.5 percent of the gross domestic product (GDP). This is not counting fines and pending litigation that ultimately will be paid for by the shareholders and employees themselves. To put things in perspective, the study notes that these costs are the equivalent of a $10 increase in the cost of a barrel of oil.[3]

It would be nice to believe, as President George W. Bush has contended, that these scandals involved only a "few rotten apples," but all evidence actually points to the contrary: that ethical and legal breaches are much more common than imagined. Unfortunately, the recent scandals reveal more than just the odd infraction; they reveal a tangled web of intertwined deceits. Executives receiving and cashing in on enormous stock options even as companies collapsed, flagrant manipulation of accounting practices, investment banks offering initial public offering (IPO) stock options to executives as a reward for using their services, and analysts trading favorable reviews of companies in return for a place at an exclusive nursery school for their daughter.

There have been many reasons put forward to explain how these types of things could have been occurring, unknown, under the nose of the other executives, the board, analysts, and the regulators. We still have few satisfactory explanations for what happened, but whatever the excuses, it amounts to an enormous knowledge management failure.

In terms of motive, no doubt much of the problem lies with the structural ties between executive pay and share value. The massive potential rewards on offer in an expanding stock market encouraged executives to engineer company earnings in the most beneficial light, concealing ownership and debt that might make investors or analysts suspicious. With enormous personal earnings at stake, executives made certain—often through questionable if not fraudulent accounting techniques—that the share price remained buoyant. Also an obvious structural concern (at least in the United States) is the dual role of CEO and chairman—an invitation for overbearing and self-serving personalities to enrich themselves and control corporate policy.

A similar structural conflict exists with the board, where corporate law dictates that directors act in the best interests of the shareholders, universally interpreted, again, to mean keeping the share price high. The effectiveness of these directors in providing independent oversight on behalf of shareholders has to be questioned with such an arrangement, particularly because most directors in large companies tend to be selected by (and often are personal friends of) the CEO. With board compensation packages ranging from $243,000 for Tyco to $535,000 for Enron, it is not difficult to see how directors could be tempted to turn a blind eye at creative accounting or unethical work practices being pursued by the company officers. Owing allegiance to the CEO and often on several company boards at once, directors said they found it difficult to question the ethics or legality of corporate policy based on limited information, particularly when the company was making record profits.

And of course, the investors themselves are not without blame. Demands for a continued high—irrationally and unsustainably high—share performance by institutional investors is what drives the entire process.

This book, though, is not about corporate scandal or structural reform of corporate governance. Those issues are complex and political, and at least in the United States will involve a stronger Securities and Exchange Commission (SEC) and a reformed and more diligent audit industry. This book is about how to prevent these types of incidents by adhering to a strong ethical framework and by improving KRM techniques.

What recent scandals do prove, if proof were needed, is that particularly in the United States, there are many incentives for business leaders to behave unethically that are built into the cultural, legal, and corporate governance framework of the modern corporation. And those same incentives—to make the numbers at all costs, not to question policy, and to choose loyalty to the company above conscience—are pushed down to employees at all levels of an organization. As later testimony by Enron employees affirmed, despite their pretense of an open and ethical corporate culture, two things were not tolerated at the company: failing to make the numbers each quarter and questioning authority. Whatever the legitimacy of their business practices, it was a cultural recipe for disaster. And, of course, these are not characteristics that are unique to only those companies that have suffered recent disasters.

This built-in "friction" in the modern corporation (something that anyone in business will immediately recognize) constantly pulls employees—including executives—back and forth between doing what is right and profitable in the long term and doing what is ethically questionable but profitable in the short term. This friction has, I contend, increased dramatically in the past decade, making it much more likely that without a diligent enterprise-wide corporate policy to manage that risk, employees will continue to feel compelled toward profit over conscience, and companies will continue to find themselves in court and on the front pages of the newspapers.

Robert Hinkley, a corporate lawyer and advocate for the Code for Corporate Citizenship, put it well, if cynically, when he said, "Companies believe their duty to the public interest consists of complying with the law. Obeying the law is simply a cost. Since it interferes with making money, it must be minimized—using devices like lobbying, legal hairsplitting, and jurisdiction shopping. Directors and officers give little thought to the fact that these activities may damage the public interest. . . . Lower level employees know their livelihoods depend upon satisfying superiors' demands to make money. They have no incentive to offer ideas that would advance the public interest unless they increase profits."[4]

What is important in the context of this book is that for each of these corporate governance catastrophes, there were two broad and consistent failures:

1. Executives and board members didn't seem to know when potential corporate governance issues were arising (a failure of knowledge management).

2. Even when they did sense that things might be going wrong (e.g., when the Enron board agreed to suspend its code of conduct to allow Andrew Fastow to create off-balance sheet partnerships), they did not feel able to act in a more ethical way (a failure of risk management and corporate ethics).

Putting aside the question of board duplicity, the fact is that hundreds of directors who are being paid significant salaries for their oversight actually seem to have no clue what the executives are doing or what is going on in the company. What is worse, even in these sophisticated and (once) profitable companies, they had no formal policies in place for determining whether those policies were ethical or risky anyway.

As many critics point out, a focus on compliance alone cannot be the answer. Accountants, within both Enron and Andersen, often legitimately disagreed whether policies were legal or not. The complexity of generally accepted accounting practices (GAAP), combined with purposely elastic phrases, means that much is left up to the interpretation (i.e., the ingenuity) of the accountants. And in many ways, getting around GAAP and SEC regulatory oversight is no different than finding ways around environmental health and safety requirements or International Labour Organization (ILO) employment practice agreements. As John Plender astutely notes in his book *Going off the Rails*, "Many investors have concluded that generally accepted accounting principles in the U.S. are a multiple choice game in which the only consistent feature is that most managers opt for whatever produces the prettiest picture."[5]

In short, no regulatory structure can be "cheat proof." After all, corporate lawyers will always be able to find loopholes in any system, and it won't take long for lobbyists to convince lawmakers to suspend or amend requirements that prove onerous or costly. It is for this reason that many of the regulatory proposals being instituted under Sarbanes-Oxley will probably not be very effective in curbing corporate wrongdoing.

The one thing that will affect executive and board behavior is a true appreciation of the long-term risks—to themselves, the employees, and the company—involved with pursuing an unethical policy. If executives don't believe that behaving ethically is ultimately the right and the best thing to do for the long-term good of both the company and the shareholders, then all the new requirements of Sarbanes-Oxley, corporate ethical statements, talk of fiduciary responsibility, and financial reports are just window dressing.

In short, aside from the need for structural and legal changes, recent scandals reveal one thing for certain: Companies need a better framework for understanding when potential policy can create an ethical conflict, whether in corporate accounts, in executive remuneration, or in operational policy. And this is dependent upon having a codified and enforced ethical standard and having a KRM framework that can provide early warning, perspective, and accurate information to corporate leaders so that they can act appropriately.

ENVIRONMENTAL POLICY

Among the several risk areas that the modern company faces, environmental issues continue to rank among the highest cause for litigation and pressure group action. Many of the world's most powerful NGOs—Greenpeace, World Wildlife Fund, Friends of the Earth—exist because of the fear of unchecked exploitation of natural resources, as international corporations continue to expand into new labor markets, encroaching more and more on previously undeveloped areas of the world. Their numbers and their influence are increasing, for good reason.

Despite the fact that most of the important environmental regulations for Canada, Western Europe, Japan, and, in the United States—the Clean Air Act, Safe Drinking Water Act—have been in effect since the mid-1970s, companies continue to violate environmental protection laws, illegally disposing of toxic waste materials and exceeding emissions limits. According to the Environmental Protection Agency (EPA), U.S. companies paid $3.89 billion in fines in 1999 and a record $4.3 billion in 2001 (more than a 90% increase over fines assessed for 1998). Violators paid more than $125 million in additional civil penalties, not counting $25.2 million paid to individual states.[6]

Apart from EPA fines, thousands of lawsuits and prosecutions are being brought in the United States each year against corporations.

There are many more that stem from illegal or unethical environmental policies worldwide. Moreover, with the Community Right to Know Act, U.S. companies are required by law to report toxic emissions. That reporting provides a level of transparency that has made many companies, in light of such public scrutiny, begin to rethink their environmental policies.

There are plenty of examples:

- Smithfield Foods and two of its subsidiaries in Virginia were assessed damages of $12.6 million for discharging illegal levels of pollutants from their slaughterhouse into the Pagan River, violating the federal Clean Water Act.
- Rockwell International, which had been fined more than $18 million in 1992 for illegal storage and treatment of hazardous waste at a nuclear plant near Boulder, Colorado, paid $6.5 million in damages to the families of two of its scientific employees who died while illegally disposing of hazardous wastes.
- When three people were killed after a gasoline pipeline rupture near Bellingham, Washington, Shell Pipeline was accused of gross negligence in its operation and maintenance policies. The accident spilled more than 230,000 gallons of gasoline into local waterways. The government is seeking more than $18 million in fines.[7]
- In October of 2000, Morton International, which produces polymers, sealants, and adhesives, agreed to pay $20 million in penalties, on top of pledging $16 million in cleanup projects, for violations of the Clean Water Act and the Resource Conservation and Recovery Act. It was found to have been not only illegally dumping hazardous wastes in offsite landfills and down wells, but of keeping two sets of records, by which it falsified its discharge and disposal activities.[8]
- Thames Water has been convicted of environmental and public health violations 24 times and fined approximately

$700,000 since 1999. In 2000 a pumping station failure allowed an estimated 22.5 million liters of raw sewage and toxic industrial waste to flood streets and homes in southeast London before flowing directly into the River Thames. The company was fined $400,000, the largest amount ever assessed under the United Kingdom's waste management law.[9]

The list goes on and on, and, of course, earlier indifference is catching up with us. In America alone, between 50,000 and 70,000 people die each year as a result of past exposure to dangerous toxins and substances. Class-action suits continue to drain companies of resources, ruining reputations for years to come.[10]

What is most surprising is that despite assertions of critics that the regulatory framework is weak and ineffectual, as can be seen from the penalty figures, regulatory agencies are fairly diligent and punishment can be very strict. The Justice Department has an Environmental Crimes Unit, and over the past decade, many of the violations have been reclassified as felonies, which entail personal punishment for executives involved. Regulatory violations now carry severe personal sanctions, and the number of criminal prosecutions of executives has been increasing over the past two decades.

Today, criminal penalties for executives found guilty of violating major environmental regulations (e.g., the Toxic Substances Control Act, Clean Water Act, and Clean Air Act) can be between $2500 and $50,000 and can carry sentences of up to a year in jail. When it can be demonstrated that executives knew that their actions were placing others in danger, individual fines can shoot up to $250,000 and involve prison sentences of up to 15 years.[11] In fact, during the first decade from 1983 to 1993, when criminal prosecutions began, individuals were sentenced to more than 380 years of prison. That amount has leapt to 256 years of prison time awarded in 2001 alone (almost double the figure in 2000).[12]

Canada too has recently seen a significant increase in the number of prosecutions against companies for environmental violations.

Pollution fines increased nearly 75 percent between 1999 and 2000 as Ontario passed its Toughest Environmental Penalties Act, 2000, which includes an environmental SWAT team, and an increase in fines for a corporation's first conviction from $1 million to $6 million (Canadian). Fines for individuals now can be up to $4 million (Canadian) per day with jail terms extended to 5 years.[13]

In developing markets, in contrast, local government regulations concerning the environment may be weak or nonexistent. For the past four decades, that indifference and lack of regulatory control has led to some outrageous environmental abuses by western—and indigenous—corporations.

These types of malfeasance are devastating to the employees, the communities, and the company but longer term, of course, have contributed to what is becoming a significant concern for companies operating overseas. There is now a broad movement of *collective resistance*—among the media, pressure groups, and increasingly customers, investors, and employees—to business generally and to American business in particular. As we have seen, the rise of the Internet, nongovernmental organizations (NGOs), and pressure groups, as well as the increasing expansion of global litigation, means that corporations can no longer pursue policies that are environmentally dangerous with impunity, regardless of the level of local government regulations.

This resistance movement, a subset of the amorphous antiglobalization campaign, is not just a concept. It is manifested in broad campaigns of scrutiny and resistance, creating more difficulties for businesses than the occasional protest or product boycott. This growing antibusiness climate can severely limit a corporation's strategic flexibility, lead to increased regulatory pressures, and ultimately affect a company's "license to operate."

In addition, as we have seen, painted with growing anti-Americanism from foreign polices, public support worldwide for U.S. business is lower than it has been in three decades. Even in the area of corruption, where American businesses might assume some level of respect, opinion of U.S. companies could hardly be worse. Despite the U.S. Foreign Corrupt Practices Act (FCPA) and similar legislation by the Organization for Economic Cooperation and Development (OECD) Anti-Bribery Convention, a recent survey conducted by the London-based Control Risks Group of companies in the United Kingdom, the United States, Germany, the Netherlands, Singapore, and Hong Kong revealed that a startling 67 percent of respondents believed that U.S. companies used middlemen to circumvent anticorruption legislation.[14] These attitudes of mistrust are confirmed with a survey sponsored by Hill & Knowlton, in which only 27 percent of respondents thought American companies were above average when it came to corporate citizenship. A staggering 73 percent rated U.S. corporations below average, and only 2 percent gave American business an excellent rating.[15]

Whether deserved or not, U.S. corporations are now associated with indifference and exploitation when it comes to environmental and human rights issues abroad. That reputation is harming individual companies, the U.S. economy, and the global economy as a whole.

EMPLOYMENT ISSUES

Developed Markets

Over the past 10 years, a series of quality and productivity movements have disrupted long-held ideas about employment and have produced formidable changes to the workplace. This is particularly true in the United States and Britain, where Business Process Reengineering, Six Sigma, International Organization for Standardization 9000 (ISO 9000), and the quality certification process, downsizing, empowerment, and part-time and flexible employment have all been successful in improving efficiency and "flattening" organizations, making them more flexible and responsive and allowing for expanded individual responsibility.

Critics, however, contend that ultimately this restructuring has come at the expense of employee loyalty and a weaker social contract between companies and their workers. Although statistics on longevity of employment are inconclusive on the subject of average employment tenure (they seem to indicate that despite everything employees remain with companies on average about as long as they did in the mid-1980s), it is certainly true to say that as a recent survey of MBA students revealed, the average employee entering the workforce no longer assumes that he or she will be with one company for life (the average is just less than eight companies before retirement).

This new employee–business relationship produces an interesting and in many ways destructive situation. Despite unprecedented new levels of responsibility and authority of action, employees today are at the same time less willing to become entangled with ethical debates or whistle blowing. With an expectation that they will move on anyway (or be fired if they say anything), a recent survey by the Aspen Institute of students who graduated in 2001 from 13 leading business schools in the United States found that the majority would simply leave the company rather than become embroiled in an ethical or legal issue that might spoil their resume, invite retribution, and bring them emotional grief. "Most MBAs indicate that they would simply opt out and find another job," the report says.[16]

And there is a further downside to this new employee–business compact. Today employees are willing to hold a company responsible for unfair employment policies in a way that would have been inconceivable just 20 years ago. Last year in the United States, there were hundreds of thousands of legal claims, including class-action suits, filed against companies for employment-related issues. Recently the Congressional Budge Office in the United States predicted a "rapid explosion of lawsuits" in the area of employment discrimination, where the current 24,000 cases in federal courts each year could leap to as many as 75,000. In the United Kingdom, where many employment-related claims are brought before employee tribunals, there were more than 100,000 appeals, a rise of 135 percent over the past 10 years.[17]

As these structural reforms to business continue and the global economy continues to falter, even in Europe and Japan, where labor regulations provide much greater job security, every company is now struggling with the challenge of maintaining good employee morale in the face of downsizing, layoffs, and a revised social contract. In fact, next to environmental violations, employment-related issues are the single most numerous cause for damage to a company's reputation.

For these reasons, corporations have to reassess the importance of employee-related policies. As Stephen Albrecht points out in his book, *Crisis Management for Corporate Self-Defense,* too often executives believe that they are separate and above employee-related concerns. The attitude seems to be that "employee problems are the responsibility of the HRD [human resources department], personnel, employee assistance, or security departments. We don't deal with those sorts of things at [the] senior manager level."[18]

However, employment issues are too important and too volatile in terms of risk to the company's reputation and bottom line, to leave to chance, or to treat as an administrative issue, with the human resources department to do the necessary paperwork. Employment-related issues need to be seen as a part of a company's risk management strategy, both because they promote greater cooperation (and therefore better productivity and risk management) and because no company wants the morale and reputation-destroying effect of legal action against it by its own employees.

As with corporate governance and financial accounting, employment is covered by a multitude of regulations. In the United States, more than in other nations, issues of diversity and discrimination are also of enormous concern to companies. Enforcement of equal opportunity employment practices usually falls to the human resources department, but poor application of these policies can be devastating. There are many examples.

Coca Cola is one of the more recent companies to be hit hard by employment-related lawsuits. In May of 2002, it agreed to pay $8.1

million to current and former female employees for salary discrimination. Combined with the $192.5 million class-action race discrimination lawsuit from 2001, the company's recent employment discrimination payouts total more than $200 million.[19]

Texaco, accused of race discrimination by six employees, agreed in 1997 to pay $115 million in settlement and $30 million more to improve the racial climate in the company. The story was carried in newspapers and on television worldwide and came on the back of a devastating recording of executives in a 1994 meeting, reported in the *New York Times,* at which executives used racial slurs against minority employees even as they discussed destroying documents linked to the lawsuit.[20]

Employment-related issues that can cause risks to a company include the following:

- Layoffs and downsizing policies
- Work-life employee and family-oriented programs
- Antidiscrimination/equal opportunity issues
- Nondiscrimination against sexual orientation
- Sexual harassment
- Freedom of association issues
- Local employment and retail site selection
- Unionization
- Living wage policies

Apart from regulation and litigation issues, of course, there is also a positive benefit to maintaining goodwill among employees. There is growing evidence that organizations that have admirable workplace polices have reaped benefits not only in terms of productivity, but also in terms of their share value. A 1999 study of 400 publicly traded companies by Watson Wyatt found that those companies with the most progressive "employee-friendly" policies had an average 5-year return of 103 percent, which was almost twice as high as companies that didn't have good workplace policies.[21]

Developing Markets

Despite recent legal action, probably the greatest up-and-coming area of risk management for companies is not employment at home, but employment policies abroad. And, oddly, given the amount of media and pressure group attention today, it is a relatively recent phenomenon.

A decade ago hardly a single company would have addressed the issue of human rights in an annual report, much less at management meetings. It wasn't that companies weren't maintaining operations—or buying from other manufacturers—overseas. But not only were expectations for social responsibility less, but the media and pressure groups were considerably less concerned with (or in a position to observe) the welfare of poor, unrepresented workers overseas.

Today, it is increasingly expected, and soon to be required, that companies build key aspects of the Universal Declaration of the Rights of Man and ILO's rights into company policies, specifically because of issues that arise from employment practices in developing economies. And, as with the environment, there is good reason to see why this has become necessary.

"We are seeing a lot of companies in the United States with sophisticated ethics programs," warns Brian R. Hollstein, a management consultant and former managing director of Decision Strategies International, "that are constantly getting surprised overseas with ethics violations."[22]

These violations are being monitored and exposed by an increasingly effective group of labor activists who now have taken the demands for good behavior one step further along a company's extended supply chain—to their suppliers in developing economies.

For companies, it has not been easy in the past to monitor what was happening in foreign markets in hundreds of factories that provide products on a completely outsourced basis. With no formal program for monitoring or enforcing ILO standards, and under pressure from NGOs and the media, companies have been forced to mobilize inspection and advice teams specifically to monitor and enforce good labor practices among these nonowned factories. GAP, for example dedicated more than 60 employees to overseas supplier inspections in 2001. Nike now deploys closer to 80, four times the number it did in 1998.[23]

In addition, although the issues surrounding wages, working conditions, and under-aged employment are usually more complex than activists at first believed, the expectations for companies have been uncompromising. Taking into account local culture and laws while maintaining a company's values and protecting its reputation with pressure groups and the investment community at home is not always straightforward. As Peter Sandman, a risk management specialist points out:

> *My multinational clients have employees and executives with a wide range of values: some who practice infibulations and some who think it evil, some who drink and some who prohibit alcohol, etc. A company that makes a special effort to hire female truck drivers in the US and refuses to hire female truck drivers in Iraq is responding to stakeholder values; a company that claims to have its own values on the matter should presumably feel obliged to standardize its hiring practices.[24]*

The problem with an approach of cultural relativism—or maybe just realism—is that it can inadvertently lead to activities (e.g., discriminating against women, overworking employees, and employing child labor) that are acceptable behavior in some developing nations, but no longer acceptable in advanced economies. As Dave Stangis, Intel's manager of corporate responsibility admits, it is a difficult issue, when dealing with the various cultural sensitivities of a global company. "Companies need to understand what diversity means in different countries."[25] There is no simple solution, of course, but again, these are the types of issues that can quickly create a crisis and therefore need to be actively and formally managed as part of a strategic risk management program.

One of the most controversial issues now on the corporate agenda is child employment. The ILO recently estimated that 246 million children—that is, nearly one in six of all children in the world between the ages of 5 and 17 years—are working. It is thought that nearly 180 million of those children work in hazardous jobs that "put their physical, mental, or moral well-being at risk." The ILO estimates that around 8 million children are involved in what the it calls the "worst forms" of child labor—slavery, forced labor, prostitution, and being forced to serve in the military.[26]

During the past 5 years and facing ugly recriminations, most western corporations initially simply made attempts to ensure that underage workers were removed from the factory's workforce. In fact, by law since 1993, the United States has officially banned the import of textiles made by children. However, as many studies have indicated, removing these children from the workforce is in itself an ethical dilemma. Turned out of these factories, children don't necessarily return to school or a well-fed and carefree childhood. With a family at least in part dependent upon their income, and quickly replaced by a teenager, too often these children are simply forced to find work elsewhere, often in even more dangerous and difficult working conditions.

Here, innovative policies by companies that pay for housing, education, and health care can not only ensure a humane response, but can also help to ensure stability and continuity of a workforce.

Chiquita provides a good example of a broader and more effective corporate response. Rewriting its code of conduct and based on the SA 8000 standard, it began working toward certification in 2000. In 2001 Chiquita began a collaborative program with banana growers to provide greatly improved working conditions for the pickers, including rebuilding facilities and initiating modern health and safety programs. Aware of child employment issues, the company helped to provide a school and day care center for workers' children and built affordable housing around the processing sites for the workers and their families. In its 2001 "Social Responsibility" report, the company lists the soft benefits that come from its efforts as greatly improved employee morale and trust. There are more measurable benefits, as well, where recycling policies have saved it millions of dollars, with savings on agrochemicals alone amounting to 14 percent, or $4.8 million a year. Similarly, something as simple as pallet recycling (before they were simply thrown away) saved $3 million, and health and safety improvements reduced costs by $513,000 per year in one division. Better worker conditions have also allowed them to avoid the perennial and crippling strikes that typically plague the industry. Plus the company also retains trained employees and essentially ensures a continued loyal workforce while avoiding underage employment.[27]

As the Chiquita example shows, as with other areas of corporate ethical behavior, it has its positive business value. Many such programs prove that with better training, legitimate work hours and good conditions, the workforce is ultimately more productive and cost-effective for both factory and buyer.

"Companies protect and enhance their brand equity by ensuring their operations—and those of their business partners—are conducted in a manner consistent with human rights principles," says Business for Social Responsibility. "Businesses are increasingly aware that they share responsibility for their suppliers' employees who manufacture, grow, or produce their goods, and recognize that they can improve supply chain management in the process. Companies working in zones of conflict are also realizing that they built their license to operate by developing practices consistent with human rights principles."[28]

PRODUCT AND WORKPLACE SAFETY ISSUES

- In December 2002, Ford Motor Company agreed to pay $51 million to settle U.S. state government claims that it misled consumers about the safety records of its sports utility vehicles and failed to disclose to the public what it knew about the Firestone tire failures, which U.S. safety regulators have linked to about 270 deaths, many from "rollover" accidents involving the Ford Explorer. The investigation by the states focused on allegations that Ford continued to use Firestone tires on its vehicles even after it had evidence of an unacceptably high failure rate and a greater likelihood of rollovers.[29]

- Following the death of an employee in a processing plant in Geismar, Louisiana, Royal Dutch Shell, the petroleum company, was ordered to pay $135,000 in settlement of charges by the Occupational Safety and Health Administration (OSHA) that it failed to comply with safety standards necessary to protect workers against exposure to hazardous chemicals.[30]

- Fisher-Price, the toy maker, agreed to pay $1.1 million to settle charges by the Consumer Product Safety Commission that it had known but had failed to reveal that its Power Wheels product could catch fire. The company had records of 116 fires and reports of 1800 incidents in which the toy maker's vehicles had overheated, short circuited, or melted, causing minor burns to nine children and causing $300,000 in property damages to houses and garages.[31]

- When *Listeria*-infected wieners killed 21 people in 1999, the U.S. Department of Agriculture (USDA) quickly traced the contamination back to Sara Lee's Michigan food plant. As revealed over coming weeks by the *Chicago Tribune,* previous USDA inspectors had cited a litany of poor inspection reports, indicating serious health and safety violations including cockroach infestation near the ovens, meat left strewn on the floor, and counters and other areas left uncleaned for days.[32]

For any company that manufactures or assembles a product, there are potential inherent risks. Those involved with product safety are real and ongoing, because usually contamination of foods, dangerous products, or poor workplace safety polices mean a breach in laws and potential harm for employees and customers. According to estimates by the National Institute for Occupational Safety and Health, each year 6000 workers are killed and 6000 severely injured in occupational accidents. Thirty percent of industrial accidents are caused by illegal safety violations.[33]

As we have seen with environmental issues, prosecutions have increased dramatically in the past few years. Within the first 8 months of 2001, the Consumer Product Safety Commission had already penalized companies more than $6 million. That amount was more than twice the total for the year 2000 and nearly 20 times the amount per year a decade ago.[34]

However, risk does not end for a company with the actual result of a product safety failure. Beyond the harm done directly and the probability of costs through litigation lies a further concern, known by Peter Sandman, a specialist in risk and reputation management, as "outrage": when consumers, legislators, investors, or pressure groups are so incensed by a company's activities that they begin an active campaign against them. Sensing negligence, arrogance, or indifference on the part of management, this outrage factor can multiply the harm to the company from a single incident many fold.

The real issue here is a combination of carelessness and isolation on the part of executives. Who could doubt that given a series of failed health inspection reports, executives would not choose to rectify the situation? The reality is that there are methods and knowledge management systems available to the average company that allow company managers to make certain that critical information on risky issues reaches them. Not to attempt to anticipate and deal with these types of risk—particularly in today's climate—is negligent and foolhardy.

"You talk to any of these executives," explains Jim Kartalia, CEO of Entegra, "they don't want to have sexual discrimination or harassment suits; they don't want to be guilty of environmental spills . . . but they don't apply the same business principles to managing risk that they do day-to-day in the quality process, so they simply don't know at the executive level what is happening in their company."[35]

BUILDING AN ETHICAL COMPANY

According to a recent survey by PricewaterhouseCoopers, "In the U.S., more than three-quarters of consumers hold companies totally or partially responsible for avoiding bribery or corruption; keeping operations and supply chains free of child labor (89.8%); preventing discrimination; protecting worker health and safety (95.4%); and not harming the environment."[36] Corporate governance, environmental policy, employment rights, and product safety are four areas in which exemplary behavior is now expected and in fact required of a company. An ethical risk and knowledge framework built around good behavior in these key areas will more effectively protect your company from devastating risk while protecting and indeed improving your corporate reputation.

Which brings us back to the three main contentions of this book. First, whether doing it because it is the right thing to do or because it is too costly not to do it personally and for the company, what is most important is that corporate executives clearly make the case for ethical behavior and then create and adhere to a formal and actionable framework for integrated ethical management.

Which brings us to the second contention of this book, which is that organizations need to know what the employees—including, it seems, executives—are doing when it comes to potential areas of risk. A quick glance at companies suffering from recent scandals makes it obvious that simply applying GAAP-required financial reporting or having an independent auditor totally failed to demonstrate to those who needed to know what was going on inside the company.

In short, corporate leaders must not simply say that they wish to behave ethically; they have to establish an integrated KRM process that helps them to know whether they are being ethically compliant or not. This requires corporations to develop a knowledge management structure that is specifically directed at monitoring and reporting on potential areas of crises.

The fact is that most serious corporate accounting debacles still come about unintentionally and arise simply because corporate leaders and decision makers lack knowledge and information about a particular situation, the options that are available to them, or the likely repercussions of their activities. In short, they come about because of a failure of knowledge and risk management.

Which brings us to our third contention: that companies need transparency and authenticity of reporting. A company should reap all the rewards possible for its efforts in establishing an integrated ethical and KRM policy, including public and investor recognition. But that recognition can come only if company policies and practices are codified, audited, and reported in a formal process. Without this formal reporting process, corporate claims may too easily be dismissed as self-serving "greenwash," or worse, if unverifiable or misleading, be used against the company by pressure groups or in litigation that contends that what the organization claims is not really true. In short, modern corporations must address key risk areas—corporate governance, environment, worker rights, product safety—in a systematic and strategic way as part of a formal knowledge management process.

CHAPTER ENDNOTES

[1] "Corporate Actions Rob Public Pension Funds," American Federation of State, County, and Municipal Employees Web site, winter 2002/2003 [excerpted from Jane Birnbaum, "Pension Robbers," *America@Work,* October]. Available from www.afscme.org/publications/primetime/pt03106.htm.

[2] Martin Wolf, "Why It Is So Hard to Fix the Flaws of Modern Capitalism," *Financial Times,* November 20, 2002.

[3] Carol Graham and Robert Litan, "The Costs of Book-Cooking," *The Christian Science Monitor,* September 4, 2002.

[4] Robert Hinkley, "How Corporate Law Inhibits Social Responsibility," *Business Ethics: Corporate Social Responsibility Report,* January/February 2002. Available from www.business-ethics.com.

[5] John Plender, "Capitalism and Ethics: What Price Virtue," *Financial Times,* December 2, 2002, p. 13.

[6] U.S. Environmental Protection Agency, *EPA Achieves Significant Compliance and Enforcement Progress in 2001* (31 January 2002). Available from www.epa.gov/epahome/headline_020102.htm.

[7] Russell Mokhiber and Robert Weissman, "Bad Apples in a Rotten System," *Multinational Monitor* 23, no. 12 (December 2002). Available from multinationalmonitor.org/mm2002/02december/dec02corp1.html.

[8] "Enforcing Federal Environmental Laws Protects All Americans," Sustainable Energy and Economic Development Web site. Available from www.seedcoalition.org/learn.epa.success.htm.

[9] "Worst Polluter in England and Wales Brings Rotten Record to United States," *Public Citizen,* October 21, 2002. Available from www.citizen.org/pressroom/release.cfn?id-1248.

[10] "Cost Justification—Environmental Health and Safety," Thomson Micromedex. Available from www.micromedex.com/products/tomesplus/chemknowledge_costjust.pdf.

[11] "Penalties Imposed by Federal Environmental Laws," U.S. National Department of the Interior BLN Training Web site. Available from www.ntc.blm/gov/learningplace/res_penalties.html.

[12] Jonathan M. Karpoff, "Environmental Violations, Legal Penalties, and Reputation Costs," Social Science Research Network Electronic Library, March 1999. Available from papers.ssrn.com/sol3/papers.cfm?abstract_id=137952.

[13] "Environmental fines up sharply in 2000," Ontario Ministry of the Environment, December 29, 2000; available from www.ene.gov.on.ca/envision/news/0089.htm.

[14] Jimmy Burns, "Laws Fail to Halt International Business Bribery," *Financial Times,* October 15, 2002.

[15] "Consumers Skeptical of Corporate Citizenship Activities," *Holmes Report,* April 25, 2002, pp. 1–2. Available from www.holmesreport.com; and U.S. Environmental Protection Agency, *EPA Achieves Significant Compliance and Enforcement Progress in 2001* (January 31, 2002). Available from www.epa.gov/epahome/headline_020102.htm.

[16] "Learning to Put Ethics Last," *Businessweek,* March 11, 2002. Available from www.businessweek.com/bschools/content/mar2002/bs2002038_0311.htm.

[17] "Employee Litigation," Tolson Messenger Web site. Available from www.tolsonmessenger.co.uk/resource/faqs/emp-lit.htm.

[18] James Altfeld, "Review of, 'Crisis Management for Corporate Self-Defense' by Stephen, Albrecht" (AMACOM Books, New York, 2002). Available from www.altfeldinc.com/pdfs/crisis.pdf.

[19] Scott Leith, "Coke Reaches Agreement on Gender Pay Inequity," *Atlanta Journal-Constitution,* May 25, 2002. Available from www.accessatlanta.com/ajc/business/coke/0525coke.html.

[20] "The Texaco, Inc. $176.1 Million Settlement: New Precedent for Race Discrimination," Web site for Cohen, Milstein, Hausfeld and Toll. Available from www.cmht.com/casewatch/cases/cwtexco3.htm; and Tammy Shaw, "Environmental Penalties Reach an All Time High," Sea Grant Law Center Web site. Available from www.olemiss.edu/orgs/sglc/high204.htm.

[21] "Workplace," Business for Social Responsibility Web site, May 2, 2002. Available from www.bsr.org.

[22] Sherry Harowitz, "A World of Possibilities," Security Management Web site, 2003, p. 5. Available from www.securitymanagement.com/library/000778.html.

[23] Sarah Murray, "Working Lives Under Scrutiny," *Financial Times*, December 10, 2002, p. iii.

[24] Peter Sandman, "Responsible or Responsive?" *Sustainability Monthly Review*, February 1999, pp. 10–13.

[25] Conference discussion by Dave Stangis entitled "Intel and Corporate, Social, and Environmental Responsibility" at "How to Manage Corporate Responsibility" seminar, October 3, 2002, sponsored by the Ethical Corporation magazine in New York.

[26] International Labour Organization, *Child Labour Presentation* (2002). Available from www.ilo.org/declaration.

[27] Jeff Zalla, "Transforming a Reputation: Chiquita and Corporate Responsibility" (paper presented at the How to Manage Corporate Responsibility seminar, October 3, 2002, sponsored by the Ethical Corporation magazine in New York); and "2000 Corporate Responsibility Report," Chiquita Brands International, Inc.

[28] "Human Rights," Business for Social Responsibility Web site, May 2, 2002. Available from www.bsr.org.

[29] Tom Brown, "Ford Settles Claims It Misled Public about SUVs," *Reuters News Service*, December 23, 2002. Available from www.planetark.org/dailynewsstory.cfm/newsid/19189/story.htm.

[30] Russell Mokhiber and Robert Weissman, "Bad Apples in a Rotten System," *Multinational Monitor*, 23, no. 12 (December 2002). Available from multinationalmonitor.org/mm2002/02december/deco2corp1.html.

[31] "Toy Maker Fined $1.1 Million for Dangerous Toys," *Houston Chronicle*, June 7, 2001. Available from www.chron.com/cs/CDA/story.hts/business/934911.

[32] Jim Kartalia, "Reputation at Risk?" *Risk Management*, May 2000.

[33] "Editorial," Multinational Monitor Web site. Available from multinationalmonitor.org/hyper/issues/1990/06/mmo690_03.html.

[34] U.S. Consumer Product Safety Commission, Office of Information and Public Affairs, August 17, 2001. Available from www.ctconnect.com/sheltonfire/NEWS%20from%20CPSCLimited-Mast%20Fined.htm.

[35] Jim Kartalia, interviewed by the author, January 23, 2003.

[36] "Surveys Find Many Consumers Hold Companies Responsible for Their Actions," from Press Room on the PricewaterhouseCoopers Web site, September 30, 1999. Available from www.pwcglobal.com.

FOUR

How Have Corporations Responded?

So what have we established? First, that the new business environment means that there are unique pressures on corporations to behave ethically in order to safeguard their reputation. New legislation in the European Union (EU) and elsewhere, combined with increased levels of litigation in the United States, greater expectations from the investing public, and active vigilance from nongovernmental organizations (NGOs) and the press, means that corporations these days must begin to rethink their strategies for knowledge and risk management (KRM). In addition to the recent emphasis on corporate governance, there are several other key areas of concern—the environment, human rights, and product safety—that every company must address strategically so that it has the capacity to sense and respond to ethical crises in these areas before they occur.

So how has the business community adjusted to these new challenges? Not all that well, in fact, although policy differs dramatically, of course, between companies, industries, and countries. Even the most respected companies often have only a rudimentary formal ethical framework. Only a handful of companies tie any process or management system to this framework that will encourage employees to adhere to that ethical code when it comes to operational, environmental, or safety (as opposed to office behavior) issues. Although there is a growing movement in Europe to adopt stringent social and environmental standards of reporting, few U.S. multinationals have adopted triple–bottom-line accounting, and most of these reports remain unaudited by an independent third party. In fact, the United Nations Environment Program (UNEP) and SustainAbility International recently published the "Global Reporters," a "Top 50" listing of multinational corporations that had distinguished themselves for reporting on issues such as environmental policy, corporate governance, and employee rights in developing countries. Only a handful of U.S. companies were represented, and these were global conglomerates (see Chapter 11).

Despite the near-universal availability and use of environmental health and safety incident management systems and decision-support software, few companies have actually attempted to integrate these systems into a formal process of KRM. A survey by Aon, an insurance broker, found that even among the top 100 European companies, only 22 percent had a formal strategy to manage brand and reputation risk.[1] For companies that have adopted knowledge management processes and systems over the past several years, these remain almost exclusively focused on coordinating operational knowledge and have not yet been adapted for identifying and managing potential risks.

In fact, most corporations have failed to appreciate the potential harm that a well-publicized incident can do to their organization. A recent KPMG survey of 35 companies with revenues of $500 million or more found that 47 percent of those companies had no crisis preparedness plan in place, even though 81 percent said they thought their companies were vulnerable to a serious operational incident.[2] Even fewer have any formal framework for identifying, assessing, and dealing with risk. A recent study by Environmental Resource Management, found that 60 percent of multinationals that they interviewed were not managing risks to reputation in a systematic way. More than a third admitted that they were not "on top of" the important issues affecting their sector.[3] These companies remain more or less in the same mindset that they have been in for the past century.

"How well you prepare for a crisis of any magnitude can make or break your organization in the marketplace if a major event does occur," says Stuart Campbell, partner in charge of KPMG's Risk and Advisory Service Practice. "Companies that emphasize recovery over planning are engaged in flawed thinking. The focus should be on preventive measures and proactive control."[4]

Although many companies have adopted some form of limited ethical framework, these efforts tend to be audit-based and focused on complying with formal regulations and laws. For others, broader operational risk management has become emotionally (and illogically) confused with a public relations exercise, with donations given to charity being used by their corporate affairs group to brand their company as "socially caring." These companies, I contend, are the ones that are not only putting their future in jeopardy, but also are undermining the legitimate nature of corporate ethical policy by pursuing "greenwash" public relations policies instead of moving toward a workable framework for risk management that will help them to avoid operational disasters in the first place.

Yet an increasing number of corporations—mostly in the petroleum, chemical, or extraction-based industries and apparel manufacturing—have led the way in terms of pioneering techniques to avoid operational and ethical disasters. Companies such as BAA, Intel or Novo Nordisk, have developed strong new approaches to risk management, incorporating advanced ethical monitoring and reporting processes and systems. Sophisticated companies that have evolved under strict regulatory regimes—defense contractors and pharmaceuticals—are also among the leaders in integrated ethics and risk management. Their techniques are valuable and worth emulating.

THE EVOLUTION OF THE ETHICAL CORPORATION

How well is your company doing? One way of gauging how well the company has responded to these new challenges is to simply chart the company's progress through four simple stages of ethical responsibility and risk management sophistication.

Stage One: The Reactive Phase

Typical of both middle-sized and larger corporations, particularly older and well-established organizations, companies in stage one probably reflect the state of affairs for the vast majority of enterprises in North America, Japan, and Europe, and probably 85 percent of all companies with a revenue of less than $10 billion. Their ethical and risk management approach is characterized by the following:

- A marketing-focused values statement and an employee code of conduct
- Ethics training limited to new employee orientation
- Varying levels of "philanthropy," usually in the form of local community charitable donations
- No formal risk monitoring or response process other than departmental operations or environmental health and safety compliance
- No real reporting on governance policies, social or environmental performance

Stage one companies are traditionally domestic-focused concerns that identify themselves with a community on which they depend for goodwill such as labor support and planning permission. Often limited in its practical value, their approach to ethics and risk management consists of a basic (usually marketing-focused) code of conduct that spells out company policy on high-level issues such as equal opportunity, consistent and honest treatment of customers, and the personal use of company property.

Although they may be large corporations with offices and manufacturing sites scattered throughout their home country, each office or plant tends to bolster its reputation locally, and so stage one companies are often focused on site-based community public relations such as local donations to charity and support of youth sports teams or scholarship programs.

Many have begun to source materials for the first time from manufacturing sites in other countries, expanding their supply chain through outsourcing rather than relocation. Their risk management approach is seldom elaborate and is usually based on being compliant with local and federal environmental, employment, and safety requirements. Limited in its effect, this framework does nothing to avoid ethical or operational disasters, and though less apt to be targeted by major NGOs than the large multinationals, companies in this phase of development account for a large and growing number of the product safety and environmental disasters that have happened in the past 5 years.

The Odwalla juice drink crisis is a good example. In 1996 a 16-month-old child died from *Escherichia coli* O157 infection after drinking apple juice made by Odwalla, a fruit drinks company. The company admitted responsibility and immediately pulled the products from the shelves, pleading guilty to having underestimated the health dangers of unpasteurized apple juice (ironically being produced because of its "natural" qualities). By all accounts, company employees at all levels, in an organization known for its strong philosophy of corporate social responsibility (CSR), were devastated by the incident.

It was only after a federal investigation, however, that it was revealed that concerns about the safety of the product and its production had been raised a number of times with senior management. Aware of an outbreak of *Salmonella* poisoning in fruit juices served at Walt Disney World the year before that had made 60 children ill, Odwalla had considered but rejected several measures for killing bacteria, on the grounds that it was unnecessary and would change the taste of the product. This was true even though the company had received complaints from customers in the past who had become violently ill. Executives decided to resort to an acid wash for the fruit, although the supplier admitted that the wash alone (without another stronger agent such as chlorine) killed bacteria in only 8 percent of tests.

Investigating the incident, Jon Entine later reported, "By summer 1996, former company officials say production demands began to over-shadow safety concerns. A contractor warned Odwalla that its citrus-processing equipment was so poorly maintained that it was breeding bacteria in 'black rotten crud' and 'inoculating every drop of juice you make.' Reportedly encouraged by executives, managers brushed aside warnings from an inspector that a batch of apples was too rotten to use—some were decayed, one had a worm—without taking special precautions against contaminants. That batch turned out to be deadly."[5]

For Odwalla the combination of poor health and safety policies and an inadequate risk management program meant that indications that should have signaled a potential crisis—badly maintained facilities, poor inspection reports, and consumer complaints—all went unheeded. This is a common scenario for companies in stage one.

Stage Two: The Public Relations Phase

Stage two organizations are usually middle-sized to large companies, often multinational, with offices, manufacturing sites, or assembly plants scattered throughout various countries. Often integrally involved with a global supply chain, buying, manufacturing, and selling components and finished product throughout the world, these companies often combine self-owned manufacturing and assembly sites with an outsourcing assembly policy. Probably 750 of Fortune 1000 companies fall into this stage. They are characterized by the following:

- Some form of corporate value statements with a more detailed code of conduct
- A strong public relations department with effective ties to local communities

- Active reputation promotion through CSR initiatives and strategic philanthropy
- Compliance-based focus on equal opportunity employment (EOE), environmental, health, and safety rules
- Multiple operational quality certifications (International Organization for Standardization [ISO] 9000; Six Sigma)
- No formal program for corporate governance, environmental, or social monitoring outside of regulatory compliance
- No officer-level positions for ethics or risk, no dedicated risk or ethics committees, and no board-level involvement in the ethics or risk management process
- No program for combining the quality standards process with risk management or nonfinancial reporting
- "Soft reporting" of social and environmental policies

Aware that the current antibusiness climate and their expansion into developing markets can bring on extra risks, these organizations have usually spent considerable money and effort in developing a strong public relations campaign, often under the heading of CSR. These companies usually have a strong community affairs program, lead by vice president–level officers, and almost universally employ a public relations firm to advise them on their relations with media and local governments and communities. Aware of the value of "cause marketing," these corporations often have a broader, more strategic program of philanthropy, usually associated with their own set of products—so pulp and paper companies have a campaign for planting trees or for encouraging recycling, and furniture manufacturers run campaigns to save the rain forests. Very often skillfully done, these efforts usually include extensive use of the Internet in this campaign, both through the company Web site and through electronic press releases.

Companies in this stage of development already have a series of compliance-based standards—based on Environmental Protection Agency (EPA), Occupational Safety and Health Administration

(OSHA), or EOE standards—and almost universally already audit their performance around these targets. These audits are limited to compliance and are usually "compartmentalized" by office or department. There is still very little relationship between auditing and reporting on compliance in these areas, and any ethics or risk management strategy. Performance improvement is seen as a separate process from the safety, environmental, or employment compliance audits, and there is seldom any attempt made to use the compliance process itself to improve productivity.

There is great merit to many of the philanthropic programs sponsored by these companies, and although the cynic might say that these efforts are primarily self-serving, these social responsibility campaigns can genuinely help those in need and benefit the community at large. Unfortunately, whatever the genuine merits of corporate philanthropy, these efforts seem to buy less tangible "good will" than might be expected.

In fact, a recent MORI survey on public attitudes revealed that despite the enormous amounts of money spent in the past 2 years on publicizing their CSR, fewer than one third (28%) of people surveyed could name a company that they thought was actively doing good, and those were mostly employees who had a personal relationship with the company. And yet nearly everyone can name companies that have done something significantly harmful. Unfortunately, the lesson seems to be that it is much more difficult to build a good reputation than it is to create a bad one.[6] And this, despite the fact that American companies increased their philanthropic giving by more than 12 percent to $10.86 billion in 2000.[7]

As part of that CSR public relations exercise, companies in this phase tend to produce claims based on what is known as "soft reporting." Using expandable phrases such as "a healthy working environment" or "a sustainable wage" in their claims, there is little rigor to their monitoring and measurement techniques and no third-part auditing to confirm their authenticity. These companies tend to "cherry pick" the issues that put them in the best light and avoid any mention of practices that don't.

In many ways, this is dangerous business, and the attempt to "green-wash" tends to undermine any genuine efforts to demonstrate improvement in these areas. "We're manufacturing lots of things that kill lots of people," satirized the Prince of Wales' Trust, "but we built three scout huts last year."[8] This is also a very dangerous position to stay in, a sort of ethical no-man's-land where the company declares that it is doing good things but can't actually demonstrate that it is true.

CorpWatch now even awards "green Oscars," for companies that demonstrate the greatest ability for "giving human rights, social, and environmental abuses a patina of respectability."[9] This half-genuine, half-marketing campaign by so many companies has had its toll on public attitudes. According to Edelman, the consultancy and market research group, the third biggest fear among U.S. consumers is "misleading and deceptive marketing practices," and only 20 percent of Americans believe or trust in corporate advertising. Only 8 percent of (generally more skeptical) Europeans have any faith in corporate advertisements.[10]

And of course, these policies do nothing to help companies to avoid reputation-ruining blunders in the first place. Enron, Coca-Cola, Global Crossing, and Texaco all had given millions in charitable philanthropy, but it didn't help them to avoid reputation-damaging incidents. What goodwill these campaigns do produce can evaporate very quickly if a disaster occurs.

Stage Three: Early Corporate Social Responsibility

Companies in stage three have taken important steps toward a combined ethical risk program and better monitoring and reporting on corporate governance, environmental, social, and product safety issues. These are progressive, almost universally multinational, corporations that come from a variety of industries. Though not exclusively large, most often companies that have reached this stage of development tend to be in the Fortune 200. Companies in this stage are characterized by the following:

- A clear corporate commitment to a high standard of ethical behavior, including a detailed code of conduct and an extensive program for ensuring employee understanding and compliance
- Measurable goals and performance indicators for corporate governance, social, and environmental activities
- Certification of quality and performance standards under ISO 9000–type guidelines
- Certification of good environmental performance under ISO 14001–type standards
- Membership in labor rights–related groups such as the Global Compact or the Ethical Trading Initiative
- Broad stakeholder involvement in developing and applying standards of social and environmental behavior
- Formal ethical sourcing requirements and supply chain inspection
- Active collection of risk-related information on trends and benchmarks
- Some form of social and environmental report, based on AcountAbility 1000 (AA 1000)–type and Global Reporting Initiative (GRI)–type standards (see Chapter 11), with a high degree of transparency
- Occasional third-party auditing

Stage three companies have moved beyond the public relations phase and have begun to include ethics and social and environmental policy into their strategic planning on an enterprise-wide basis. That strategic approach also combines broad certification efforts in quality and process standards such as ISO 9000 or Baldrige, as well as certification to environmental and social standards such as ISO 14001 or Social Accountability 8000 (SA 8000). These companies are usually actively engaged in collaborative efforts to promote high employment standards through groups such as the United Nations' Global Compact and through regular social audits of employment policies throughout their supply chain.

Most will have a chief ethics officer and a formal program for communicating and enforcing high ethical standards throughout the company and down the supply chain through suppliers. They have usually developed a strategic policy that reflects their shift from shareholder value to stakeholder value. They have also begun to emphasize personal employee responsibility for ethical behavior, occasionally through sophisticated incentive and reward systems. They will have a confidential hotline and written policies concerning employee confidentiality and protection of whistle-blowers.

Many of the companies in this stage have begun to integrate their reporting efforts in financial and nonfinancial areas, usually using the Global Reporting Initiative, and will have some degree of independent third-party auditing. They are beginning to see meeting social and environmental standards as a way not only to boast about their progressive policies, but also to begin to improve productivity and efficiency through conservation and re-use policies.

Yet, despite their good efforts, most organizations at this phase of their evolution still will not have made the leap toward integrating triple–bottom-line reporting and KRM techniques into their ethical framework. Each of those areas are still seen as separate and unique, and these companies still have seldom made an effort to develop a corporate-wide approach to risk management—where the ethical framework, application of standards, and an active risk management process are integrated with a corporate-wide knowledge management process to provide organizational leaders with an "early warning system" for responding to ethical and operational risks (Figure 4.1).

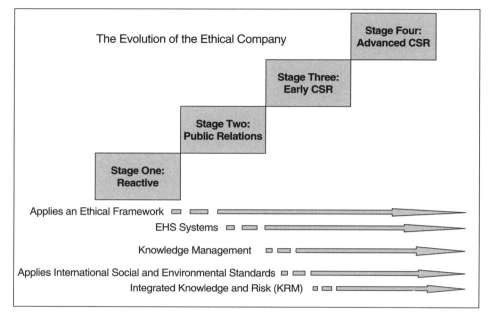

FIGURE 4.1 *Four Stages of the Evolution of an Ethical Company*

Stage Four: Advanced Corporate Social Responsibility

Today occupied only by a few highly progressive organizations, this stage of advanced CSR finds companies moving toward the ideal integration of the several key processes—active ethics management, applied international standards, accurate and audited social and environmental reporting, and integrated KRM—that when combined provide a company with a strong ethical risk management framework. Although there are many companies moving in this direction, most have successful implementations of several, but not all, of these key initiatives. Only a handful of organizations have fully integrated those processes into a strategic ethics risk management process. Companies in this stage have several of the following characteristics:

- A chief ethics and risk management officer, board-level participation in the ethical and risk assessment process, and a

dynamic program of ethical communication, education, and incentives for employees at all levels
- An integrated framework linking KRM and ethics as part of a company strategy
- Integration of quality management certification with financial and nonfinancial reporting and certification
- Support for broad "aspirational initiatives" such as the United Nation's Global Compact
- Use of triple–bottom-line accounting as a strategic operational tool
- Full transparency and third-party auditing
- A strategic view of the purpose of their company that goes beyond just profit, incorporating ideas such as "full life-cycle" product responsibility, and includes open involvement of stakeholders throughout the supply chain

Natural Selection

These are simply high-level categories, and it is often the case that a company may well be more advanced in one area than another. Although only a couple of companies are in phase four—and they have pursued this level with some determination—the vast majority of companies remain in stage one or two. Yet, given increased pressures and new opportunities, there is no doubt that the direction for most organizations is ineluctably toward higher levels.

Reflecting this inevitable move toward stages three and four, PricewaterhouseCoopers has some interesting predictions:

- Within the next 10 years, the valuation methods used by Wall Street analysts will include new metrics—such as social performance and intellectual capital—to assess more accurately the net worth of a company.

- Within the next 5 years, 70 percent of North American and European companies will assign board responsibility for areas of reputation and social responsibility.
- Within the next 10 years, the majority of global multinationals will publish a broader range of key nonfinancial information alongside financial data, covering areas such as environment, diversity, community development, and anticorruption.
- The future credibility of audits will depend on the audit firm's ability to review and give opinions on nonfinancial performance, inevitably in conjunction with nonaudit professionals, including NGOs.[11]

One thing is certain for the vast majority of companies that are contentedly in stage one or two: It will increasingly be a risky and uncompetitive position to be in over the coming years. These companies in stages one and two are going to have to do more to safeguard their reputation than simply give away money and boast of support for community development. Whatever the merits of such philanthropic activities, a genuine program of ethical risk management requires much more of a company than just developing good public relations and boasting of "social responsibility" on a Web site.

Call them fickle or demanding, but neither the press nor the buying or investing public will be swayed much by the temporary "feel-good" factor that comes from a corporation's donations to charity or executive pronouncements about concern for global causes. At best, such philanthropy will buy your corporation some "goodwill" credit if your organization is found to be exploiting children, violating employee privacy laws, or involved in an environmental disaster. At worst, an organization risks being seen as insincere and manipulative—guilty of using charity and corporate responsibility pronouncements as "greenwash"—even while pursuing more cynical policies of exploitation.

The good news is that even as expectations for corporate behavior have risen, so has a company's ability to avoid disasters in the first place. Valuable ethics management techniques, information systems, and knowledge management practices are available, and for many companies, these are already part of their operational focus. And emerging standards for triple–bottom-line accounting, beyond their value for boasting of good performance, are based on process and performance standards that help a company—in their very implementation—to closely and continuously account for and deal with the types of threats in product safety, environmental, or employment policy that can cause a company great harm.

All of this, however, does mean that corporate leaders will need to rethink the way their company is approaching their ethical framework and may require reorganizing systems and processes specifically to focus on preventing ethical and operational disasters. Understanding how to address and avoid these types of disasters is increasingly becoming part of strategic planning in the modern world and requires sophisticated knowledge management techniques. Companies can begin that portion of the process by assessing at which of these levels they need to be, determining where they are now, and planning how to get to where they want to be in the future.

Chapter Endnotes

[1] Alison Maitland, "The Value of a Good Reputation," *Financial Times,* March 30, 2003.

[2] Stephen Taub, "More Corporate Crimes and Misdemeanors," CFO.com, September 16, 2002. Available from www.cfo.com.

[3] Alison Maitland, "The Value of a Good Reputation," *Financial Times,* March 30, 2003.

[4] Stephen Taub, "More Corporate Crimes and Misdemeanors," CFO.com, September 16, 2002. Available from www.cfo.com.

[5] Jon Entine, "The Odwalla Affair—Reassessing Corporate Social Responsibility," Jonentine.com, January/February 1999. Available from www.jonentine.com/articles/odwalla.htm.

[6] "Is Industry Socially Responsible?" MORI Surveys, November 25, 2002. Available from www.mori.com/polls/2002/kar-csr.shtml.

[7] "The American Association of Fundraising Counsel's Giving USA Report" [as cited in "Consumers Skeptical of Corporate Citizenship Activities," *Holmes Report,* April 25, 2002, p. 2]. Available from www.holmesreport.com.

[8] "The Responsible Century?" Prince of Wales Business Leaders Forum, 2000. Available from www.pwblf.org.

[9] Vanessa Houlder and Alan Beattie, "Shades of Green," *Financial Times,* August 19, 2002, p. 10.

[10] Richard Edelman, "Rebuilding Public Trust Through Accountability and Responsibility," (paper presented at the "How to Manage Corporate Responsibility" conference, October 3, 2002).

[11] Surveys Find Many Consumers Hold Companies Responsible for Their Actions," from Press Room on the PricewaterhouseCoopers Web site, September 30, 1999. Available from www.pwcglobal.com.

PART TWO

A Program for Corporate Integrity

FIVE

Moving Beyond Stage Two

So how does a corporation move beyond stage two? What do companies need to do in order to embed an ethical approach to corporate governance, environmental and employment policies, and product safety into their core business processes so that it is a natural part of their day-to-day business operations?

As leading practices from companies in stage three and four demonstrate, the best way to create that unique combination of a strong ethical culture while avoiding unethical or illegal accidents is to initiate a formal enterprise-wide process incorporating an ethical framework and internationally accepted reporting standards, with a knowledge management program for monitoring all areas of risk. These, when integrated with quality improvement standards and existing environmental health and safety (EHS)–type processes, provide the most successful approach to an overall ethics and risk management process. In addition, as some large companies have found, the combination of due diligence and reporting that comes with this type of process can also contribute to the quality and process improvement within an organization, thereby creating productivity and efficiency gains.

In fact, there are several important principles that we have learned from the business improvement revolution of the past two decades that should be incorporated into this next evolutionary step for businesses. These well-known principles include the following:

- Organize your company on a horizontal (i.e., process) rather than a vertical (functional silo) basis.
- Empower employees with greater decision-making authority, and with that authority, personal responsibility for quality and productivity improvement.
- Use systems, as much as possible, on an integrated and enterprise-wide basis to collect information and communicate important business knowledge to employees.
- Actively manage and measure performance.
- To make a strategic organizational policy stick, use a long-term organizational approach, rather than a project-based approach.

From these broad principles have sprung many of the most important management initiatives that have occurred in modern business, including business process reengineering and the broader quality movement that today requires certification with International Organization for Standardization 9000 (ISO 9000)–type standards as a minimum. Similarly, theories behind the value of empowerment created many of the important aspects of change management, including the broader use of teams and a more effective application of incentives and rewards. Companies need to leverage these principles in order to take the next step up to stage three.

There are other advancements that have come to companies in the past decade that have made it easier for an organization to move beyond stage two. One important characteristic of most stage two companies is that they already have a good deal of enterprise-wide change management experience from a combination of recent Enterprise Resource Planning (ERP) and quality initiatives such as ISO 9000.

At the same time, ERP and other powerful software platforms have moved companies ineluctably (if painfully) toward better systems and information integration and sharing, as well as better collaboration between areas such as planning, production, maintenance, accounting, and sales. And, of course, the knowledge management movement rose from the combination of these new technologies and more collaborative organizational policies, including efforts to capture and leverage the important information and knowledge that exists throughout the corporation. It has been a significant struggle, and though not universal, most companies have come a long way toward completing most of these broad restructuring programs that make a company look at its operations in a more integrated holistic manner. It is now time to take the next step by applying those same principles to an integrated program of knowledge and risk management (KRM).

The integrated risk management movement is the next step in the quality movement, contends Jim Kartalia of Entegra. "When the quality management movement began it was slow getting started in the U.S.," he remembers. "Employees said, gee, I don't want to report defects, I might get in trouble."

"But business leaders forced a big cultural change, explaining that they were going to embrace quality management—they were going to get ISO 9000 certification—and they turned to the employees for help. They provided the reporting systems and training, and spent a lot of money."

"But America was better for it—we produce better products now and better services," he concludes. "This is the same thing. It requires a cultural change—more than just the window dressing of a CEO signing a piece of paper."[1]

The Ethical/Risk Framework Decision Process in the Typical Corporation

Because most companies have developed mechanisms for preventing ethical or legal violations on an "as needed" basis, prompted by various infractions and incidents over the years, most organizations have never considered ethics and risk management to be a single strategic process. In fact, one of the greatest inhibitors of detecting and avoiding risk is that companies today still often have the same sort of silo-based compartmentalization that plagued other operational processes in the past.

This means that there is little coordination between corporate functions and reporting systems, and no attempt is made to create a formal "early warning" process for identifying potential reputation-damaging incidents. Ethical codes and value statements are introduced to new employees and remain primarily within the domain of human resources and the legal department and are never mentioned again (until an incident occurs). Environmental safety still has a compliance-based focus, lacking full integration into operational improvement, risk management, or strategic planning. Most corporations still have a variety of methods to help them avoid product safety, environmental, or employment crises, yet these methods remain piecemeal and uncoordinated and are usually established only on a departmental level, varying widely in their implementation between groups. Companies seldom use integrated enterprise-wide systems or processes to record incidents, capture trends, or conduct regular reviews by senior management.

All this means that most companies in stage one or stage two have created multiple areas of focus that have developed throughout the organization to address risks. Typically, these areas of focus include the following:

- A written ethics policy consisting of value statements and rudimentary behavior guidelines administered by the human resources department
- Processes for incorporating Occupational Safety and Health Administration (OSHA), Environmental Protection Agency, and ISO requirements and audits in the manufacturing and delivery process, administered by the operations and supply chain functions as part of a Process Safety Management (PSM) regime
- Employment issues dealt with exclusively within the domain of human resources

- Strategic planning in charge of advising on corporate strategic policy
- Chief financial officer and audit committee to address accounting concerns and financial compliance
- A corporate legal office to address legal compliance issues
- A board of directors to provide the highest level of oversight

The problem with this approach is obvious. *First, there is usually little coordination between these areas.* Operations, quality, sales, accounting, internal audit, health and safety, environmental management, human resources, executives, the board: All of these areas tend to remain relatively separate on a day-to-day basis.

This fragmented approach is common to most organizations. "For too long," says Lynn Drennan, head of the Division of Risk at the Caledonian Business School at Glasgow Caledonian University, "the practice of 'risk management' has been compartmentalized within organizations. Health and safety management, fire prevention, security, internal audit, insurance, and business continuity planning have often been placed in separate little boxes, creating tensions between, rather than working in harmony with, one another."

The normal processes that help a company to detect potential crisis issues are usually focused on manufacturing and product safety and are pursued through day-to-day operational policy that is initiated through OSHA and EHS standards. Some companies have instituted environmental safety systems, but these too are usually seen as separate from an overall ethical or crises response policy framework.

"For many organizations, risk management is piecemeal, uncoordinated, and focused exclusively at an operational level," concludes Drennan. "What is needed is a more holistic approach to 'risk management.' One which understands that these functions are interrelated and that a change in one can have an impact on the others."[2]

Making things more difficult is that in most organizations, the emphasis on ethics begins and ends with a values statement hung on the cafeteria wall and a high-level code of conduct that is signed and forgotten after new employee orientation. Not only is there little corporate emphasis placed on ethical behavior or concern for the company reputation, but there are no workable standards or guidelines to which the average employee can turn in order to assess risk or act on issues.

True, human resources professionals will be aware of federal guidelines in terms of equal opportunity employment or sexual harassment, but they are seldom involved when a company is making the decision about whether to work with a factory in Guatemala that may employ underage workers in unacceptable conditions. Even when shop floor operations have EHS compliance increasingly built into their processes, these activities are usually based on a "minimum compliance" model and little valuable information is captured or learned from the process. Legal understands high-level regulatory requirements, but most environmentally related decisions are made by mid-level managers in the field with little substantive policy guidance. Audits are usually still exclusively finance focused, and particularly in foreign or nonowned factories, audits are either nonexistent or cursory and almost never include employee or environmental issues. In short, there is no coordination between the various parties whose opinions may be needed in order for the company to make the best decision on a controversial issue.

Second, not only are these activities uncoordinated, but there is little corporate oversight. Typically, each of these departments is perceived as a specialist silo, with a leader that is keen not to be seen doing something wrong in front of his or her peers or to reveal uncomfortable issues to his or her superiors in the organization. With no formal audit or review process and no pervasive ethical code of conduct, too often employees are encouraged at a departmental level to sweep incidents under the carpet. These incidents go unrectified and unrecorded.

Ironically, in most large companies (as we have seen repeatedly during testimony in the 2002 scandals), the board members have little knowledge or understanding of potentially reputation-threatening issues; there is no formal mechanism, other than possibly the financial reporting–focused audit committee, through which these issues are brought to their attention. Ultimately responsible for oversight of company policy, too often board members have little operational information upon which to assess potential risks to the company's reputation.

"Typically," says Jim Kartalia, "what we have seen is that there are departmental information silos where the information is really only contained for that one department and every department has a different information system—whether it is a regulatory compliance or incident management system—and there is no overall consolidated enterprise approach."[3]

In most companies, general council becomes the coordinating party. But lawyers, usually risk averse and with little operational knowledge, focus on compliance issues and cannot be expected to advise on broader public reaction issues; the sort of issues that though not illegal may cause enormous public outrage. Moreover, in our "can-do" culture, operations and sales people are often hesitant to take an ethical or risk query in front of legal council, assuming that they will be "putting their head on the chopping block" and that the answer to any query will invariably be "stop doing whatever you are doing."

Third, this type of approach is almost exclusively internally focused. With many incidents, the outrage that a policy might cause is not obvious to internally focused employees. To truly judge potential policy risks, companies need formal and active contact with a variety of stakeholders, from NGOs to suppliers, taking into account the important shift that stage three and four companies have made from shareholder to a broader stakeholder focus. This shift in emphasis from a focus exclusively on shareholder value to a broader focus on stakeholder value is one of the more important characteristics of a stage three company.

For the past two decades, the concept of shareholder value has been central to Anglo-American business. In management consultancies in the 1990s, the walnut-paneled offices of the "big five" echoed with the mantra "shareholder value" with a determined singleness of purpose. The idea is that companies are actually owned by and responsible to the shareholders, and therefore the primary duty of management is to increase the wealth of those shareholders (with the unsaid implication that all other parties involved—employees, local land owners, or endangered species—are of secondary importance).

What is often not appreciated, though, is that achieving the greatest profit for the shareholders in the long run may be dependent upon a more balanced approach to management in which other groups (stakeholders) are taken into account. These stakeholders include customers, environmentalists, NGOs, regulatory agencies, local communities, the government, and even, many would argue, future generations (Figure 5.1).

The explanation for this phenomenon is obvious to those who appreciate the problems involved with risk and reputation management. Whether employees, auditors, NGOs, or suppliers, stakeholders will have an important effect on how a company manages its risk

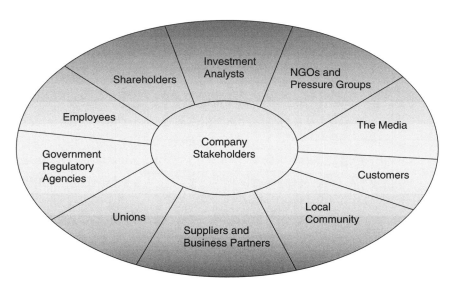

FIGURE 5.1   *Various Stakeholders in the Modern Enterprise*

and avoids incidents that result in fines, litigation, loss of reputation, and consumer boycotts. Their cooperation and input is key to understanding potential risks to the company. This is why, in terms of developing an integrated ethical risk management program, it is important to incorporate the expectations of the various stakeholders into the process as closely and effectively as possible.

Fourth, an uncoordinated and local approach to risk management is both static and reactive. Without a coordinated and predetermined risk review process, a company simply waits for an incident to arise and then reacts as best it can. There is nothing about this type of organizational approach that provides the agility or structure that is necessary to be able to predict when crises are about to occur or to deal with them proactively.

Finally, most companies are still not taking advantage of the systems and procedures that are available and commonly used throughout the corporation. Most companies in the past decade have adopted important new enterprise systems, such as ERP, supply chain management and sourcing software, environmental management systems, intranet groupware, and knowledge management software, that can be integrated as part of an ethics and risk management process. Those systems can be used to contact early alert teams, to instantly and accurately inform key decision makers and experts of the key issues, to help assess legal, societal, and environmental implications, and to coordinate the decision-making process.

KEY ELEMENTS OF THE MODERN ETHICAL FRAMEWORK

The most effective approach to an enterprise-wide KRM process seems to incorporate several key aspects that take companies well beyond the public relations model and incorporate most of the practical aspects of the "stage three, Early CSR" approach, combined with the best techniques learned from business process reengineering, change management, and knowledge management in the past.

- First, an organization needs a coordinated well-managed program specifically focused on an ethical management framework. This usually means an ethical framework consisting of board- and senior-level leadership, a dedicated ethics and risk management center of excellence, a chief ethics risk officer, a value statement, corporate conduct guidelines, and an education and communication process, incentives, and punishments.
- Second, companies advancing into stage three need to institute an integrated KRM process. This means creating a dedicated knowledge management process that leverages best-practice risk and knowledge management procedures and systems from the shop floor to the board. This process must be based on the knowledge management technologies and new organizational and managerial procedures that have been used so productively in the past decade. As part of that strategic process, a company also needs to integrate risk processes and systems that are today often stand-alone and uncoordinated. The ability to mobilize the knowledge and expertise of company employees and to provide them with accurate and real-time information about potential crises is key to a proactive risk management process. This also means using systems to help take advantage of the information that is available within the corporation, from stakeholders and from external research and analysis.
- Third, reflecting the adage that "you can't manage what you can't measure," a company needs to adopt performance standards that provide for the level of due diligence and review that will allow decision makers to accurately assess risk and to respond quickly and appropriately. These process and performance standards must be internationally recognized and auditable. They will provide the process and performance measurement basis for focusing procedures on social and environmental issues, and most particular, risk in general.

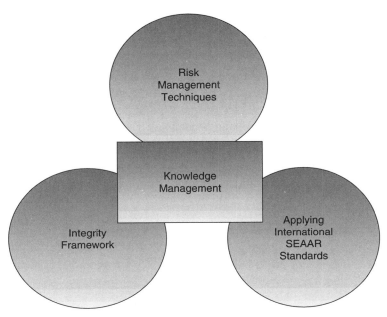

FIGURE 5.2   *An Integrated Knowledge and Risk Management Approach to Corporate Integrity*

They will also need to be integrally tied to the company's values statement and internal code of conduct.

- Fourth, a company moving into stage three will want to adopt open, transparent, verifiable reporting on "softer" nonfinancial subjects using triple–bottom-line accounting and reporting techniques.

An Integrated Knowledge and Risk Management Approach to Corporate Integrity

Together these four key components make up an organization's KRM framework. These components need to be applied using many of the better ideas developed in the past decade concerning integrated information systems, communications, knowledge sharing, and an overall mechanism for capturing and distributing information concerning potential risks from those who know to those who need to know.

CHAPTER ENDNOTES

[1] Jim Kartalia, telephone interview with the author, January 23, 2002.

[2] Lynn Drennan, "Risk Management: A Holistic Approach," *Risk Management,* 11 November 2001, p. 1. Available from www.riskmanagement.com.au.

[3] Jim Kartalia, telephone interview with the author, January 23, 2002.

SIX

Establishing and Managing an Ethical Framework

An ethical framework is a combination of procedures and written guidelines that help a company to actively manage its ethical behavior, and through that behavior, its risk. It is predicated on the idea that the best way to deal with an ethical dilemma in the modern corporation is to avoid it in the first place. To do that, a company must ensure that its employees—from the board to the shop floor—recognize when something is unethical, illegal, or potentially damaging to their corporate reputation. Beyond this, employees at all levels have to see it as their responsibility to act on these types of issues. It is critical that the company makes it as easy and effective as possible for its employees to do this.

WHERE MOST CORPORATE ETHICS PROGRAMS FAIL

The idea of managing corporate ethics, of course, is not new. Most companies have some sort of ethical framework, usually based on ethical value statements and a short introduction to corporate ethics that takes place during new employee orientation. Nearly 75 percent of all U.S. companies have a code of conduct, and about one third of all corporations with 500 employees or more offer some sort of introductory ethical training.

Given the continuing number of corporate incidents, are these codes of conduct simply ineffective? To a large extent, yes, particularly if not coordinated with a fuller risk management process. There are many reasons for this. An ethical policy fails if:

- Employees feel that ethical conduct is relative, depending on the trade-off between that behavior and the amount of potential profit to be compromised.
- Executive leadership seems to endorse ethical behavior in name only.
- The values statement and code of conduct address only narrow, self-evident issues.
- Ethics is mentioned only as part of formal employee orientation, giving the impression that it is nothing more than a legal requirement.
- Bringing a potential problem to light is seen as demonstrating disloyalty to management or a lack of dedication to company success.

Ultimately, the value of a corporate ethical framework comes not from telling employees what is right and wrong at a generic level (employees usually know this anyway). Codes of conduct, value statements, and newsletters, as important to the framework as they are, do not usually change behavior or encourage reporting of potential issues. After all, nearly every company—even those that have recently been found guilty of the most egregious violations—had some form of written code of ethics. Enron, for example, had a chief ethics officer, a code of conduct, and a value statement that pledged themselves to "communication, respect, and integrity." This approach did little to prevent the illegal and unethical activities that brought about the company's ignominious collapse.

The ethical framework really becomes valuable only when employees feel both that they understand what constitutes an ethical risk and that they also feel comfortable and personally obliged to bring that risk to light. For this reason, probably the greatest value of an ethical framework is that when done well, it demonstrates to employees that the company genuinely cares about ethical behavior and is willing to invest time and money in order to ensure that illegal or unethical incidents don't occur. Such a framework becomes the structure for communicating values and principles that help employees to judge whether their behavior or everyday issues present a risk to the company. It does this in several ways.

First, and most obviously, the very process of developing the framework helps the company leadership and employees to think through what values are most important to them as an organization and provides an objective reference guide for making decisions.

Second, a framework demonstrates to employees that the company's desire is genuine and efforts are real. This type of framework provides a "visible" standard that forms the basis for expressing both a company's desire to behave ethically and a guideline for that behavior.

Third, creating an ethical framework demonstrates to the outside world that efforts are being made, something that is increasingly important both legally and practically if risk incidents do arise. As pointless as a value statement or a code of conduct can be, if it is ignored by executives and not taken seriously by the company culture, a corporation is at much greater risk if it has no value statements or written codes of conduct at all. In fact, as we will see in a moment, one of the most important reasons for a formal approach to ethics and risk management is that without one, company employees, including the most senior executives, risk both criticism and more often increased personal liability for their actions.

Finally, an ethical framework serves as a skeleton around which a company can implement an effective risk management program. The key elements—dedicated personnel, written codes of conduct, ethical guidelines, and specific policies concerned with reporting and confidentiality—are the basis upon which a company begins to actively monitor and respond to potential risks.

JUST WHAT IS AN ETHICAL FRAMEWORK?

An ethical framework is a significant undertaking, and to be effective, at a minimum it should include the following:

- A corporate ethics office lead by a chief ethics officer
- A board-level ethics committee
- A corporate value statement
- A code of conduct providing detailed guidelines on behavior and procedures for notification, among other things, with scenario examples and a clear statement of penalties
- A strong program to communicate those values and guidelines to all employees
- A mechanism, usually at least a confidential "whistle-blowers" hotline, for communicating employee issues
- Clear and effective monitoring and enforcement procedures

The Corporate Ethics Office and Chief Ethics Officer

Successful companies, ethics professors, and risk management professionals all seem to agree that there are two fundamental requirements for an effective program of integrated ethics and risk management. The first is genuine commitment by senior leadership. The second is for the employees at all levels—from the board to the shop floor—to feel that they are ultimately responsible for managing risk and ensuring ethical behavior.

One thing we have learned from enterprise-wide change projects such as Enterprise Resource Planning or Business Process Reengineering before it is that success depends on strong, visible, and active leadership. In fact, many studies (including one, ironically, by Arthur Andersen) find that the most important component of a successful ethics program is how the employees view senior management's commitment.

As an example, an Ethics Resource Center study that surveyed employees in U.S. companies in 2000 found that employees said that their own behavior was influenced most by their supervisors. "We found a strong connection between employees' perception of their leaders and their own ethical behavior," says Josh Joseph, a researcher from the center.[1]

It is not just the leadership aspect; there is an organizational logic as well. After all, chief executive officers (CEOs) and board members for most companies are the only individuals who have not only personal responsibility, but also organizational control, over various divisions, each of which may be making decisions that conflict with overall organizational policy. Unethical practices that can harm a company can happen in many areas of an organization—financial, operational, or sales and marketing—and only the most senior corporate officers have a view of all of these various activities.

Many progressive corporations have also established an office for risk or ethics management, directed by a chief ethics officer, chief corporate social responsibility officer, or chief risk officer, depending on the tone and emphasis of the project. Chiquita and Intel have corporate responsibility officers, British Telecom has a head of sustainable development and corporate accountability.

This position calls for a recognized organizational leader; someone who has the political presence and personality to act as a liaison between employees, the CEO, and the board. Duties include helping to create and manage the company's integrated ethical framework, to set the tone of urgency and determination, and to communicate policy to all employees. The chief risk/ethics officer needs to be invested with significant authority, to be able to deal with every constituency, and to press forward with an investigation of potential misconduct even when there seem to be political ramifications. This means often serving as the first level of screening for an incident or acting as an ombudsman for complaints or a whistle-blowing incident. They will usually also be responsible for setting up or at least advising on ethical measurement and performance indicators. In short, it is a tough job.

In the past, this position has too often been filled with a more junior leader, without either the personal or the organizational authority to

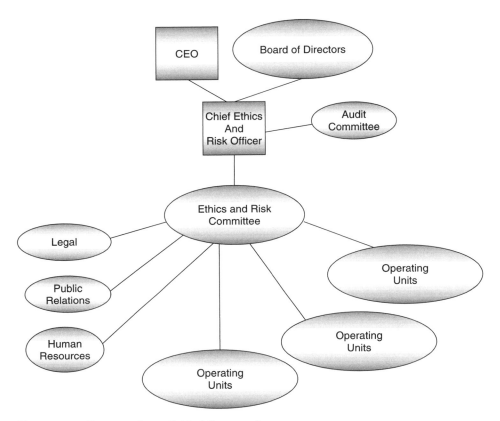

FIGURE 6.1 *Resources for an Ethical Framework*

act quickly and effectively in recognizing and bringing risks quickly to the most senior management. Too often, too, they remain still closely identified with a particular function in the company and lack the level of political independence necessary to act on behalf of the entire company. This not only makes the role ineffectual but also sends out the wrong message to employees: that ethics and risk management are not a "chief officer" concern.

The role of this internal ethics and risk office is to drive the process forward on a day-to-day basis, helping to communicate policies to employees, to integrate risk management techniques (see Chapter 8) into operational and decision-making processes, and to monitor and rank any pressing issues that arise, elevating those issues quickly to senior management and the board-level ethics committee. Their activities and responsibilities include the following:

- Implementing ethics and risk management policy throughout the organization
- Communicating ethics and risk policy among employees and stakeholders
- Developing education and training programs
- Providing guidance and advice on ethical and risk issues
- Confirming and monitoring compliance, adherence/oversight
- Directing the "risk" scanning exercise
- Tracking and resolving identified risks
- Reporting directly to board or corporate ethics committee

A Board-level Ethics Committee

Many stage three corporations have formed board-level committees to review the company's ethical policies or potential ethical hazards on a regular basis. The idea that this level of activity should take place at the board level, given the potential harm done by uncontrolled risk, is justified. After all, the role of directors in a modern company is to review strategic plans, proffer guidance on difficult issues, and assess the overall success of senior leadership and the progress of the company. Possible ethical or public relations debacles should be seen as a natural part of that role.

Recent scandals have revealed just how isolated and uninformed many board members can be and the dangers of having board members who are aloof or too high-level, afraid to understand and wrestle with key corporate policies. It is a tricky balance to be achieved between remaining too strategic and yet not falling into the unhelpful habit of micromanagement.

Part of the problem is that many board members simply don't understand the intricacies of the company for which they are supposed to provide oversight. "Unfortunately," observes Constance Horner, guest scholar in Governmental Studies at the Brookings Institute, "many companies, especially smaller ones, provide better orientation for employees in the mailroom than they do for directors in the boardroom."[2]

Moreover, it is not just the good of the company that is at stake. Today, board members often find themselves in a position of personal liability for failing to properly monitor the activities of the companies on whose boards they are serving. "It is ironic and amazing that there is a true lack of knowledge by a majority of Directors and CEOs, and a common reason why a high percentage of boards are not run well," contends Charlene Miller, founder of the International Corporate Directors Institute and Global Associates. "Most Directors and Officers do not understand the risk and exposures they are liable for."[3]

This trend toward holding board members personally responsible for failing to provide a proper level of oversight began in earnest in the United States with the announcement in 1991 of the Federal Sentencing Guidelines for Organizations, which provide a strong incentive for companies to adopt formal programs to oversee ethical and legal compliance. The guidelines were issued by the U.S. Sentencing Commission, a small federal agency that sets criminal and corporate penalty guidelines. These guidelines reduce criminal fines (up to 95%) for corporations charged with ethical or legal violations that can demonstrate that they have a formal and "effective" process for oversight in place.

Effective is generally interpreted to mean that companies have a written and well-communicated code of business conduct, and that the process for oversight is managed by a senior organizational officer. They must have in place a comprehensive employee ethics training program and complete employee background checks when hiring. They also need to provide a confidential "whistle-blowing" mechanism for employees, and they must demonstrate that they have made an effort to identify, report, and take action on (and prevent in the future) illegal activities.

The obvious effect of the guidelines has been twofold. First, they allow corporations to avoid penalties for criminal activity that come about because of a rogue employee. But companies—and boards—can avoid responsibility for that employee's action only if they can demonstrate that they had taken "reasonable" care as company leaders to avoid those illegal activities and that the employee's actions did not reflect corporate management's "systems, values, or culture."[4]

More important, at least to board members, is that the guidelines set in place a requirement for directors themselves to ensure that their company has such a risk management process in place, or risk personal liability. Directors' responsibility was further heightened in 1996 by a ruling in the Caremark shareholder–led lawsuit that found that members of the board of directors of a company had a legal obligation not only to ensure that an "effective system" of risk management was in place but also to actively supervise the activities of company managers as part of that risk review process.

"A director's obligation," declared the court in its decision, "includes a duty to attempt in good faith to assure that a corporate information and reporting system . . . exists and that failure to do so under some circumstances may . . . render a director liable for losses caused by noncompliance with applicable legal standards."

According to Chancellor Allen, head of the Delaware Chancery Court that adjudicated the case, "The Guidelines offer powerful incentives for corporations today to have in place compliance programs to detect violations of law, to promptly report violations to appropriate public officials when discovered, and to take prompt, voluntary remedial efforts."

This means that a company's ethical framework should be "reasonably designed to provide to senior management and to the board itself timely, accurate information sufficient to allow management and the board, each within its scope, to reach informed judgments concerning both the corporation's compliance with the law and its business performance."

Importantly, the court saw it as the duty of directors to make certain that the company had that type of ethical/risk framework in place, concluding that "a director's obligation includes a duty to attempt in good faith to assure that a corporate information and reporting system, which the board concludes is adequate, exists, and that failure to do so under some circumstances may, in theory at least, render a director liable for losses caused by non-compliance with applicable legal standards."[5]

This landmark decision means that board members now, potentially, can be held liable for failing to adequately supervise corporate employees who commit criminal and civil offenses, particularly if it can be shown that the company has made no effort to put a formal ethical framework in place.

This type of legislation is not unique to the United States. Australia, for example, enacted a similar federal law that came into effect in December 2001, which required companies to implement a formal risk management program within 6 months or face serious criminal penalties or fines. Board members and executives, and the company as a whole, now face criminal penalties, fines, or seizure of property "if it can be shown that the organization had a corporate culture that ignored the new legal requirements to manage risk."

"Under the new Commonwealth laws," according to Standards Australia, "a company convicted of many offenses in a wide range of areas, including safety standards, child sex tourism, slavery, drug trafficking, and perverting the course of justice, will have fines of hundreds of thousand of dollars—and by reason of having a conviction, be forced out of key businesses such as financial operations."

"Companies must take action immediately to ensure they meet the full requirements," according to Ross Wraight, chief executive, Standards Australia International (SAI). "Ignoring risk is like sleeping on a time bomb."[6]

And yet, despite these potential concerns for board members and the executive team, only those companies in stages three and four (i.e., companies that are mostly in the Fortune Global 250) have the sort of integrated ethical and risk management frameworks that the court is suggesting.

"If I were asked to sit on a corporate board, among the first questions I would ask the CEO is 'Does your organization have a code of conduct? Do you have a corporate ethics and compliance program in place? What does it consist of? How is the board informed of issues in these areas? Do you have a code of conduct for the board?'" advises John Nash, immediate past president and CEO of the National Association of Corporate Directors in Washington, D.C. "I strongly encourage companies to develop and implement effective corporate ethics and compliance programs."[7]

In fact, pressure on board members to oversee the ethical behavior of their companies does not end there. One of the more compelling ideas to come out of recent scandals is that insurance companies are now beginning to raise their premium fees—or in some instances refusing to provide coverage altogether—to board members and company officers if a company cannot demonstrate (through the sort of reporting and management techniques that are advocated in this book) that it has a proper risk management framework in place.

The American Insurance Group, for example, announced in the fall of 2002 that they would provide "a new form of liability insurance for independent directors. The product specifically extends protection to board members' personal assets."[8]

This coverage may not be so freely extended to directors in the future. In another twist to the concept of insurance-driven ethics, directors at Qwest and other corporations under fire for potentially risky business practices were told by their insurers that they were at risk of having their liability insurance rescinded.

As William Gamble of Emerging Market Strategies points out, corporate governance is a risk issue. "Like all other risks in the marketplace, it can and should be managed by the market."[9]

If insurance companies continue to lose money because of board members' indifference, there will soon be a strong incentive for board members to hold their organizations accountable, if only because insurance companies themselves will want to be certain of minimizing their own risk. The Association of British Insurers, with this in mind, now ask companies to explain in their annual reports what steps they have taken in order to manage social, environmental, and ethical risk. As a result, nearly two thirds of Britain's FTSE 100 companies are now providing some level of disclosure in these areas.[10]

In the end, if a company cannot get good board members because the insurance industry sees the company as too risky to provide liability insurance for directors, there may be a scramble for companies to prove that they are lower risk. That will require the sort of framework we are describing here.

Still, as Professor Lynn Paine of Harvard Business School recently noted, there is concern that too much of the pressure for reform is being focused on the boardroom. Directors need to be diligent, he concedes, "but if we don't have the parallel and required changes in the actual management practices, I don't think the best board in the world can carry out all the responsibilities we expect of them."[11]

Although it is too early to see how directors will be affected by recent scandals, one thing is certain: Board members should be concerned with the ethical and legal activities of company employees. The surprise is that given the potential consequences, so few corporations have established these types of formal programs.

A Corporate Value Statement

Everyone in business is familiar with the corporate mission statement, and most people quite rightly find it of little value. It is a marketing tool, and not a very good one at that.

In contrast, a corporate value statement is something different and can be a potentially valuable part of establishing an "effective" system of oversight and compliance as mandated by Caremark and other guidelines and legislation. The value statement puts into words the principles that corporate leadership expects. As ineffectual as that may sound, it is still important, for both the executives and the employees, for several reasons.

First, it forms both the tone and the logical premise of a company's program of integrated ethical management, getting down on paper a description of what values are important to the organizational leaders.

Second, it forces company officers to think about why the company exists. This may sound contrived, but the answer may not be as obvious as it seems (i.e., for many companies, it is not always and only to make a profit the next quarter). In the past few years, executives have been focused almost exclusively on keeping the company's share price high, by financial manipulation, misreporting, and sheer hyperbole. As the recent scandals have demonstrated, quarterly financial results are only one way—and not always a perfectly dependable way—of measuring success. Corporations need to also think about how they are managing change in the global economy, and how they are protecting their assets and their corporate reputation over the long run.

There are many good examples of worthwhile value statements. CSR Europe, the Brussels-based business and nongovernmental organization (NGO) collaboration network, has looked at many types and recommends something along the following lines.

"The company shall operate in compliance with all applicable laws, rules, and regulations relating to various licenses, labor, wages, worker health and safety, environment, and all other relevant laws. The company shall treat all workers with respect, dignity, and fairness. The company shall operate in such a way so as to minimize the impact of its processes on the environment. The company management shall be committed to put in place an effective system to ensure it conducts business in a socially responsible manner."[12]

Johnson & Johnson pioneered this type of ethical framework and has had its "credo" for nearly 30 years. That credo explicitly defines its priorities: Customers are placed first, suppliers and business partners second, employees third, local communities fourth, and shareholders fifth. It is a refreshing inversion of the idea that shareholder value can be narrowly defined; the company has had consistent above–market share returns for its investors over those three decades.[13]

That credo proved invaluable in the 1980s when seven people in Chicago died after taking cyanide-laced Tylenol capsules. Ignoring advice from attorneys and consultants who contended that a product withdrawal might imply company guilt and harm the brand name, Johnson & Johnson managers immediately called for all Tylenol products to be removed from the shelves, even before they consulted the CEO (who turned out to be on an airplane at the time the story came out).[14]

David Clare, company president at the time, recalled that the credo provided a clear set of principles for action:

"There were literally thousands of decisions that had to be made by on the fly every single day by hundreds of people around the organization. And we give great credit to the credo in helping them make the right decisions because they knew basically what was expected of them. We said, 'You make the decision—whatever it is, whatever it costs us—on the basis of whatever our responsibility is.' And it worked."[15]

As with Johnson & Johnson's credo, the value statement should also take into account the needs of your various stakeholders—employees, customers, shareholders, and the wider community. And unlike the mission statement, a value statement usually does not focus on "making highest returns for our shareholders" or being "a leader in our industry." The value statement usually instead focuses on the relationship the corporation wants to have with its employees, customers, and the broader community and stresses the importance of ethical business practices, or the company's relationship with its employees or the environment.

On the other hand, these value statements can't be too "apple pie" or they become meaningless. What is more, as we have noted before, these statements are only as good as the real intentions of senior management and serve a purpose only if they are part of a wider program.

Too often we have seen valuable words misused. Enron, after all, claimed that integrity was a core corporate value, vowing in its value statement to "work with customers and prospects openly, honestly, and sincerely."

A Code of Conduct

A code of conduct is different from a value statement in that it provides more detailed guidelines on behavior and procedures for notification. Often with scenario examples and a clear statement of penalties, it makes core principles and expected standards of behavior more explicit.

Surprisingly, given their value and given the precedent set by U.S. sentencing guidelines, codes of conduct are still far from universal in companies. Only about two thirds of U.S. companies have a written code of conduct, and a survey of 178 British companies completed by the Institute of Business Ethics found that even among the companies that did have a code of conduct, many of the most important aspects were omitted; one third of companies had no procedures for whistle-blowing and did not give a copy of their code to every employee. Only one third of British companies made their codes available to the public.[16]

Like a value statement, but in much greater detail, a code of conduct provides specific guidelines for behavior and sets out standards of practice. As evidence of its importance, at Enron the board of directors was asked to waive the company's code of conduct in order to allow the off-the-book company creations and partnerships that were their undoing. The fact that the board willingly gave dispensation to Andrew Fastow and others to disregard the code of conduct, ironically, demonstrates in many ways the value of the code itself.

A code of conduct, at the right level of detail, provides employees with a guideline for day-to-day behavior and is an important part of an integrated framework that demonstrates, both legally and publicly, the level of corporate maturity. It should therefore go well beyond simple statements about attitudes toward personal and professional integrity. It should also address any areas that are explicitly illegal and easily interpreted, such as taking or giving bribes or employing under-age workers. Ideally, the code should cover all the things we have been considering, including acceptable behavior for specific issues concerning the following:

- Billing and contracting
- Safety
- Selling and marketing policies
- Behavior with customers
- Adherence to quality and testing requirements
- Discrimination, working hours, child labor, coercion, freedom of association, and other work-related issues
- Wages and benefits
- Health and hygiene
- Use of company resources
- Environmental policy
- Political contributions
- Corporate privacy policy
- Board independence, terms of service, and compensation for directors

Ultimately, of course, each company will want to create a code that matches its own unique set of issues and culture. As part of the company's overall communication process, the code should be openly distributed to all employees and stakeholders. A good code should also include specific descriptions of enforcement and confidential reporting mechanisms such as "whistle-blowing" procedures, as well as the specific resources available to employees to discuss and clarify issues confidentially.

As we have seen, having this type of code of conduct in place is becoming mandatory. The New York Stock Exchange, for example, as of 2003 was planning to adopt new requirements for listing companies, which include a code of business conduct that addresses issues related to financial trading and securities, including conflicts of interest, fair dealing, and executives' use of personal property.

It is probably worth a note of caution about the development and distribution of the code. Human resources and legal departments too often are seen as the logical "owners" of the process, particularly if the company does not yet have a dedicated chief ethics officer or an ethics committee. However, as many companies can testify, there can be problems with this approach.

First, it is important not to convey to employees the sense that the ethics process is simply something that is done because it is required or advisable by law. All codes have a tendency to either remain at too high a level, where they are little more than detailed value statements, or at a level of granularity that makes them seem to be compliance based. A good code is supposed to serve a greater purpose than simply requiring employees to do the minimum required by law.

Second, even if administered by human resources, there is a danger that employees perceive the code as an initial employment-related issue, and not a day-to-day operational matter. A total ethics and risk management strategy is dependent, above all, on having employees incorporate good ethical analysis in their everyday behavior.

The Ethics Committee

Depending on the size and scale of the corporation, there may be a separation between the board ethics committee and a more operationally focused corporate ethics committee.

The most effective ethics committees usually reflect the independent structure of the company's audit committee, combining independent directors, senior leadership, legal counsel, human resources, and representatives from many of the different functional areas within the company. This level of broad representation is necessary in order to keep the board from being dominated by any one (usually legal or human resources) representative. In any case, the board members must do more than simply evaluate or approve the ethical framework itself. They should be active members of an ongoing management review process, helping to identify potential areas of risk, reviewing oversight procedures, and understanding the mechanisms for anticipating, evaluating, and reacting to potential risk issues. They should consider it part of their function not only to review the business case for major ventures, but also to be concerned with any significant proposal that involves health, safety, employment, or the environment.[17]

Reporting to the ethics committee, some progressive corporations now have set up a number of formal "risk/ethics teams." Usually comprised of employees from many different functions, these teams normally include line/operational expertise, trained risk managers, and representatives from legal, public relations, finance, and human resources. These standing committees tend to be broken down into logical areas of concern, such as the following:

- Workplace health and safety
- Employment/human resources
- Insurance
- Environmental policy
- Public relations
- Audit
- Major projects
- Product development

These kinds of risk analysis teams, though expensive in terms of resource and time, are extremely valuable not only because they help to communicate and inculcate good ethics/risk management behavior throughout the organization, but also because operationally these types of multifunctional teams tend to provide invaluable perspective on risks and consequences. They are often the best way to help expose risks at their earliest stage. As we will see in later chapters, these expert teams are an important part of a company's knowledge and risk management (KRM) framework, serving as a bridge between a company's ethics and risk management processes.

There are several good examples of this type of employee-inclusive approach. Novo Nordisk, a leader in developing this type of advanced ethical framework, translates its values directly into "commitments" that are in turn part of the performance criteria upon which the company judges its success. Adopters of triple–bottom-line reporting, they also use a balanced scorecard approach to assessing their performance. A committee of 17 senior organizational leaders systematically review this process along with the values and principles on a regular basis. Based upon hundreds of interviews and workshops with employees every three years, they essentially rework the framework from the ground upward, based on that feedback.[18]

"This job didn't exist at Intel in 2000," says Dave Stangis, Intel's manager for corporate responsibility. "What has happened in two years is a broadening understanding within the company that we have the systems and people in place to deal with these issues. We have meetings with the directors of purchasing, EHS [environmental health and safety], legal, and corporate governance, and so there is now a key network of people that understand that we have the process to manage issues this way."[19]

It is also important that companies make it as easy as possible for employees to adhere to this ethical framework. One way of doing that is to provide very clear guidance about how to discuss concerns or to report possible ethical violations confidentially. This means a clear statement for each employee of how to report to human resources or the ethics committee with assurances of confidentiality and anonymity. At a minimum, this should include a confidential "hot line."

Monitoring and Enforcement Procedures

Finally, it is important to clearly spell out the need for "zero tolerance" when it comes to ethical violations. It is a difficult policy to promote well, because listing punishments and threats of enforcement tends to frighten employees and disrupt free flow of knowledge and ideas about possible questionable policies or behavior. And, of course, it is difficult to assess before an incident the level of guilt, responsibility, and punishment. Nonetheless, it is very important that every company employee appreciates the fact that the company is serious about enforcement. For that reason, companies usually put in a statement of how the policies will be enforced, what the penalties will be, and how the process of punishment will be followed.

Guiding Principles for an Ethics Framework

There are a few guiding principles that are worth considering when developing an ethical framework.

- The ethics framework, including the values statement and code of conduct, should be written, endorsed, and communicated by executive leadership. Carly Fiorina, CEO of Hewlett-Packard, provides a good example, declaring that "good leadership means doing the right thing when no one is watching."[20]
- The code of conduct must be applied and understood by all employees, at every level in the company. In the first instance, this can be done through effective education, communication, and training, but ethics and risk management policies are ultimately most effective when they are made integral to the employees' day-to-day work. Make certain that every employee receives and signs a copy of the code of conduct. Equally important to communicating company values and expectations, though, is soliciting input from employees. Many companies hold employee survey and focus groups as a way of soliciting input and buy-in from as many employees as possible during the rollout phase of the program.

- Extend your process to include suppliers and vendors. Beginning with your tier one group of suppliers, discuss your ethical policies and have them agree to and sign a copy of the guidelines.
- Make participation in some active form of risk management part of the requirement for all management positions.
- Address strategic issues. If the ethics framework is going to take on a broader more strategic function and become the groundwork for an enterprise-wide program of risk management, it should not be limited only to issues such as the dress code, honesty in the workplace, sexual harassment, and treatment of customers.
- Make certain that both with the messages delivered in the communication program and through a confidential hot line employees realize that they can report or discuss issues confidentially and without fear of retribution.
- The ethical framework should be both locally applicable and global in scope. This may require variations in policies or phrasing, depending on cultures and laws, and it is always valuable to include international personnel during the development process.
- Finally, the program should be built not upon the minimum standard, but on the most stringent policy if a conflict between industry standards and local laws arises.

AN ETHICAL COMMITMENT

However contrived and unfamiliar it may seem, this level of focus on ethical behavior is actually invaluable to a company. Almost universally, this type of approach forms the framework for a broader policy of risk management and corporate social responsibility that characterizes those companies that have progressed beyond stage two.

The advantages of this type of formal and written approach to ethics are not just for employees, of course. It is equally valuable to company leaders, because it provides both a context and a common language for addressing ethical issues. This can be important when wrestling with difficult discretionary situations or when explaining difficult decisions to peers and subordinates. Employees need to see that company leaders have considered the underlying ethical issues— such as integrity and reputation—and not just the business drivers of quarterly profit.

As with quality production or information, the ethical process in a corporation can't simply be left to chance; it has to be organized and managed. Nor can it simply be a compliance-based "bolt-on" process done to provide a veneer of respectability. As with Johnson & Johnson, ethical behavior and risk management need to be something that is integral to the company's way of working.

Ultimately, as important as this ethical framework is, alone it only qualifies a company for stage two, a level that today increasingly constitutes the minimum standard in the modern corporation. It is certainly a prerequisite of any move toward stage three or four, as it forms the backbone of processes, policies, and resources that are necessary for an effective company-wide program of integrated KRM.

Because values have a way of making their way downward through an organization, companies in stages three and four claim that the most critical factor in a successful ethics framework is the support of the senior management team. There needs to be a broad and genuine belief that ethical behavior, according to the code, is best for the company no matter what the scenario. Executives have to genuinely believe that doing what is right is not just another way of making short-term profit, avoiding litigation or bad publicity. They must believe that ultimately ethical action is always the best course. If not, all of the effort is for nothing.

CHAPTER ENDNOTES

1 Heesun Wee, "Corporate Ethics: Right Makes Might," *Businessweek,* April 11, 2002. Available from www.businessweek.com/bwdaily/dnflash/apr2002/nf20020411_6350.htm.

² Constance Horner, "Creating and Sustaining the Strong Director," *The Brookings Institute,* Winter 2002. Available from www.brook.edu/views/articles/horner/2002winter_dab.html.

³ Charlene Miller, "The Need for Educated Change in the Boardroom," *Larta,* November 4, 2002. Available from www.larta.org/lavox/articlelinks/021104_cmiller.asp.

⁴ Win Swensen, "Companies Themselves Are the Best Crime-fighters," *Financial Times,* September 2, 2002.

⁵ "Effective Compliance Programs Can Protect the Board of Directors," *Integrity Interactive.* Available from www.integrity-interactive.com/compliance/mkt_expertise_pg5.htm.

⁶ "Risk Management—Global Trends and Experiences," *Standardisation Connection* 9, no. 1 (January/February 2002). Available from www.standards.org.sg/files/vol9no1art1. htm.

⁷ Victoria Wesseler, "Corporate Board Membership: Risky Business," Ethics and Compliance Strategies Web site. Available from www.ethicscompliance.com.

⁸ Amity Schlaes, "On the Board, A Good Man is Hard to Find," *Financial Times,* November 19, 2002.

⁹ William Gamble, "Insure Against Corporate Malfeasance," *Financial Times,* December 5, 2002.

¹⁰ Alison Maitland, "The Value of a Good Reputation," *Financial Times,* March 30, 2003.

¹¹ Andrew Hill, "A Year of Scandal," *Financial Times,* December 30, 2002.

¹² "Model Code of Conduct," CSRWorld Web site. Available from www.csrworld.net/modelconduct.htm.

¹³ Simon London, "The Third Way for Business Priorities," *Financial Times,* December 18, 2002.

¹⁴ Heesun Wee, "Corporate Ethics: Right Makes Might," *Businessweek,* April 11, 2002. Available from www.businessweek.com/bwdaily/dnflash/apr2002/nf20020411_6350.htm.

¹⁵ Thomas White, "Ethics Incorporated: How America's Corporations Are Institutionalizing Moral Values," Center for Ethics and Business, Loyola Marymount University. Available from www.ethicsandbusiness.org/corpeth.htm.

¹⁶ "Ethics Codes/Values," Business for Social Responsibility white paper. Available from www.bsr.org/bsrresources/whitepaperdetail.cfm?documentid=395.

¹⁷ Thomas White, "Ethics Incorporated: How America's Corporations Are Institutionalizing Moral Values," *Center for Ethics and Business,* Loyola Marymount University. Available from www.ethicsandbusiness.org/corpeth.htm.

[18] Vernon Jennings, "Managing Sustainable Performance at Novo Nordisk," (talk presented at the "How to Manage Corporate Responsibility" conference, October 4, 2002).

[19] Dave Stangis, interview with the author, January 23, 2003.

[20] John Plender, "Capitalism and Ethics: What Price Virtue," *Financial Times,* December 2, 2002, p. 13.

SEVEN

Understanding the Value of Knowledge and Risk Management

For stage three and stage four companies, effective risk management is not only dependent upon a strong ethical framework; it is equally dependent upon a company's ability to sense potential risk issues, to analyze the situation using the skills and expertise of its employees, and to respond in a measured and effective way. To do that, a company needs to marshal the information and knowledge that is available to it, both inside and outside company walls. That process is *knowledge management*.

WHAT IS KNOWLEDGE MANAGEMENT?

As we have seen, in order to really understand what potential risks a company is facing, it needs to actively manage the information that comes from this process in a strategic way. In short, a company needs to apply a combination of knowledge and risk management (KRM) techniques in order to use the ethical framework and international standards as part of an overall risk management policy. In fact, a company *can't manage its risk today without managing its knowledge.*

Knowledge management is a term that describes the process by which a company organizes, collects, shares, distributes, and learns collectively from employees, stakeholders, and the outside world. It is a broad framework for actively managing the information and knowledge that is available to it.

The knowledge management movement actually had it roots in the 1970s when a number of management theorists, including Peter Drucker in the United States and Humphrey Sturt in the United Kingdom, argued that as industrial society progressed, it would naturally move toward a higher skill service economy in which knowledge (i.e., what is inside employees' heads) would play an increasingly important role in innovation, productivity, and economic growth. In the 1990s, the movement saw a resurgence when a plethora of management theorists, including Nonaka and Takeuchi who wrote their best-selling book *The Knowledge-Creating Company* in 1995, began to apply theories about actively managing this knowledge on an organizational basis.

The importance of the concept of knowledge management is that it makes explicit many of the things that we know intuitively about the way a company works—that it is the cooperative application of what employees know that allows a company to create innovative new products, to solve complex problems, to do things efficiently, and in stage three and stage four companies, to help sense and respond to risk.

The knowledge management movement, however, has had more than its share of teething problems, mostly because from the outset a schism developed among those who saw knowledge management as primarily a function of collaboration between humans (the high-touch side) and those who believed that sharing of knowledge was made possible mostly through technology (the high-tech side).

This high-tech versus high-touch quarrel continues today, with proponents writing, lecturing, and arguing over esoteric ideas of tangible versus intangible assets, who owns knowledge, and whether knowledge is traded in a "knowledge market." The high-touch group contends that only organizational change can create a "knowledge-sharing and knowledge-creating culture," leveraging the skills, understanding, memories, and creativity of employees. The high-tech group argues that what organizations really need is to be able to adopt better data-management and data-mining techniques and to expand on the way information is collected, organized, and made available to employees electronically.

Much of this discussion is worthwhile and could have been applied usefully, were it not for the fact that the business press quickly latched on to knowledge management as "the next big thing" and then proceeded over a 5-year period to overexplain the subject and overhype the potential benefits. In what some have called the "in-flight magazine" phenomenon, thousands of managers and organizational leaders stormed back to the office contending that if they "only knew what their company knew," their organization would achieve an enormous competitive advantage. Managers attended hundreds of conferences worldwide, books and articles were churned out, and business school seminars dissected every nuance of the theory.

In fact, despite its critics, and apart from the more esoteric applications, the basic tenets behind knowledge management—that a company needs to actively manage the knowledge and information that it has available internally and externally—actually proved to be very practical. So practical, in fact, that much of what was argued as revolutionary in knowledge management theory just 5 years ago is today fully absorbed in the way organizations function on a day-to-day basis.

In fact, knowledge management techniques are widespread and commonplace among companies today. Today intranets and company portals, complex data mining, knowledge repositories, groupware and e-mail, skills databases, and knowledge-mapping techniques are nearly universal among progressive companies. On the high-touch side, communities of practice, after-event reviews, and the capturing of lessons learned are also commonplace in this type of organization. Presentations, project plans, and other key documents are sent freely among employees by e-mail, and the intranet itself allows employees to easily access company policies concerning benefits, ethics codes, and other important issues.

The adoption of these standard knowledge management techniques is born out by recent BSI surveys in the United Kingdom that found that 80 percent of U.K. organizations already engaged in knowledge management and 96 percent believed that they would in the next 5 years.

Even in 1999, Pricewaterhouse Coopers (PWC) annual survey of chief executive officers (CEOs) found that 97 percent of senior executives believed knowledge management was a critical issue for them. A similar survey by KPMG in Europe found that of the 100 largest companies, 87 percent of senior executives were either considering or actively engaged in knowledge management projects at the time.[1]

These same techniques are now being applied by stage three and stage four companies to leverage information and employee and stakeholder knowledge in order to better manage risk. That risk management, as with knowledge management, comes in both high-touch and high-tech components. For example, sensing and responding to risks in an organization is very much dependent upon this same intellectual capital (i.e., the knowledge and judgment of employees at all levels). Employee insight—in terms of anticipating potential accidents, a personal recollection from a similar incident in the past, a story swapped weeks ago around the coffee machine that can alert a supervisor to an impending manufacturing line incident or environmental accident—all can keep a disaster from occurring. But that knowledge is much less effective if left to filter through a management structure in a haphazard way. It needs to be actively managed and encouraged in a way that helps employees to see that this type of knowledge sharing of insight and ideas is an employee's responsibility and an ethical duty.

Similarly, the "high-tech" aspect of knowledge management, in terms of intranets, groupware, predictive, decision-making, and incident management tools, is available to the modern corporation. Browsers and search engines allow organizations to understand what is happening in the outside world, and how that information relates to their organization, in a way that was inconceivable just a few years ago. Today organizations can easily monitor or pay others to monitor for them what political or cultural factors should be taken into account when proposing policy or a project, what the competition is doing, what the media, nongovernmental organizations (NGOs), or local population or opinion leaders are saying about the company and its policies.

"Since risk management is primarily about using previous knowledge and producing and integrating new knowledge—whose quality is affected by the quality of knowledge management—you can see that risk management is dependent on knowledge management," says Joseph Firestone, chief knowledge officer of Executive Information Systems.[2] And as Simon Lelic, senior editor at *Knowledge Management* magazine points out, "Those organizations that have developed effective, KM-based processes and ways of working are also less likely to be exposed to risk in the first place."[3]

Knowledge Management Procedures and Techniques

Possibly the best way to understand what is meant by knowledge management in the context of a risk management framework is simply to look at some important knowledge management techniques and procedures.

Knowledge Mapping

Knowledge mapping is a process by which an organization determines "who knows what" in the company. It has many forms, including skills mapping, where employees list specialty knowledge and project experience, which is then captured in a relational database and made available through the company's knowledge management portal. Sometimes known as "knowledge yellow pages," this skills and experience mapping allows a company to understand where experience and expertise lie in the company and where needed skills or knowledge may be missing.

An extension of this idea is the use of an "accountability matrix" by which those employees who are responsible for making decisions or supervising tasks are mapped and tied together electronically through a relational database and software application so that responsibility for project decisions can instantly be accessed when an important decision needs to be made quickly.

Communities of Practice

"Communities of practice" are naturally forming networks of employees with similar interests or experience or with complementary skills who would normally gather to discuss common issues. In knowledge management, communities of practice are actively identified, and members of these networks are encouraged to gather and exchange ideas on a formal basis, capturing lessons learned, swapping ideas, and sharing insight. This formal management of an informal process helps an organization to create a company culture in which knowledge sharing is encouraged and opinions and ideas flow more freely among departments and offices.

"Hard-tagging" Experts

Hard tagging is a knowledge management process that combines knowledge mapping with a formal mentoring process. As part of the knowledge-mapping and skills-mapping process, experienced employees are identified or "hard tagged" so they will become part of a consultation pool that will be available when special advice is needed on developing incidents. These "hard-tagged" specialists also team in communities of practice with "soft-tagged" employees—those who are interested in learning specialist skills or in sharing experience—in a mentoring and knowledge-sharing exercise.

Textron, for example, the U.S. conglomerate, has identified and trained a group of 500 "black belts" who are experts on efficiency and who act as both intermediates and advocates for a knowledge-sharing process that encourages employees from around the corporation to share best-practice ideas openly with other employees in other sites.[4] This type of hard tagging, when done well, is much less expensive and much more effective than formal classroom-based education, bringing together communities of employees with similar interests and experience and helping to keep lessons learned, memories, and experience circulating "in the company" even as employees move on or retire.

Augmenting the Decision-making Process

Making information and experience available to company leaders during an incident or potential crisis is critical to the decision-making process of risk management. Decision making in an advanced risk management process should involve consultation with an incident management team, made up of a group of experts from a community of practice or a knowledge network, who are best able to analyze, debate, and help agree on a course of action. The decision-making process therefore becomes much better informed and balanced, with contributions from people who understand the situation, from experts who have experience with similar events, from those who can advise on scenarios and plans for resolution, and from the decision makers themselves. Access and speed are often crucial to the success of incident management decision making, so electronic knowledge mapping is used to bring together critical information to team members and to notify deputies in the event that a hard-tagged specialist is not immediately available. As Lynn Drennan, from Glasgow Caledonian University observes, "The old cliché that 'knowledge is power' applies here. Only with good knowledge management will an organization, and its employees, have the quality of information that it requires for effective decision making."[5]

Learning

One of the most important tenets of knowledge management is that employees should share experiences and techniques with others in the company so that there is a continuous and dynamic process of knowledge sharing and learning taking place. "After-event reviews," such as those used in the military and many leading companies these days, help specialists to debrief and "postmortem" incidents—learning from both what they did right and what they did wrong in the situation.

One of the greatest benefits from this process of postincident assessment and continuous learning is that employees digest "lessons learned" from previous mistakes, and that problem resolution doesn't each time require "reinventing the wheel." The mentoring aspect of hard tagging, meetings within communities of practice, and formal exchange of best practices all contribute to not only a better informed workforce, but to retaining a corporate memory, helping to ensure that incidents don't reoccur.

Possibly most important, this process of formal, company-advocated knowledge sharing sends the important message to employees throughout the organization that they have responsibility and authority to voice concerns and act on ethical, legal, or safety issues that might harm the company.

Encouraging a Knowledge-sharing Culture

Central to the success of a KRM framework is the concept that values and expectations for ethical behavior must be communicated widely and effectively throughout the organization. Integrity has to become part of the corporate culture. This needs to be done as part of this process for knowledge sharing, of mentoring and formal ethics training, so that employees at all levels appreciate the importance of good behavior. This means there needs to be regular and consistent communication on values and processes that encourage sharing of ideas and early identification of risks.

"Knowledge management," suggests Simon Lelic, "can go a long way to helping businesses achieve this ideal, where workers at every level are actively involved with minimizing an organization's exposure to adverse risk."[6]

"A couple of years ago we put in place a global tracking system," explains Dave Stangis, Intel's manager for corporate responsibility, "for managing emerging issues that looked at the top ten or eleven issues under corporate responsibility." This issue-tracking system is based on a URL site that is available to all employees and addresses issues such as human resources, legal, community issues at production sites, corporate welfare, environmental health and safety, product impact, product ecology, the social aspects of the company's technology, investor relations, governmental affairs, market impacts, and political contribution. Building on their long-standing "right to know" policy, the site is a source for questions or comments from employees anywhere in the world on these issues and provides the company with important insight on emerging issues and risks, which are automatically directed to company experts and leaders. The site is also used to post answers to employee questions, to explain Intel policies, to provide relevant articles, and contact information on content owners and company experts. In addition, each week Stangis' department provides more than 100 key experts in the company with a summarized newsletter on emerging issues. It is an effective two-way program of communication and issue identification and resolution.[7]

In fact, as we have seen, most serious incidents can be prevented if detected early and brought through a formal process to executive decision-makers or the board. But this early detection is dependent upon employees "on the ground" sensing and responding to early warning signs that in their experience indicate a potential incident. A company needs to formally encourage a process for communicating these values and to encourage sharing of ideas and concerns generally.

In addition, given the problems inherent in "whistle-blowing," even in a company culture that encourages this type of preventive concern, it is important that a company provide a balanced combination of incentives and sanctions that will help to temper the "make the numbers at all cost" culture that pervades many organizations.

Information Technology Systems

As part of the "high-tech" aspect of knowledge management, a company should now be using information technology (IT) systems—Enterprise Resource Planning platforms, customer resource management and call-center technologies, or environmental management systems—to help capture trends or early indications of a risky operational situation developing. Stage three and stage four companies have often also purchased specialist incident management or risk management software (see Chapter 10).

There are various knowledge management software solutions that help a company to identify experts, to collect and distribute important information, to capture lessons learned, and to complete business research and analysis. Possibly more important, the communication and organizing features of the modern intranet, groupware, and relational database technologies need to be used to help capture, organize, and distribute relevant and time-sensitive information about key performance areas, risks, or opportunities to those who need it in a timely way. This needs to be done using information management rules concerning priority and timeliness in order to overcome the massive "information overload" that can mean critical risk information is never acted on, lost among hundreds of e-mails or project updates.

Performance Monitoring and Reporting

Underlying a successful knowledge foundation is the need to measure, monitor, and boast of organizational performance. This has been part of the "measures that matter" movement that began in earnest with knowledge management several years ago, in which nonfinancial performance information, including intellectual and organizational capital, is used to predict the future success of a company. In keeping with the move toward greater transparency and better nonfinancial reporting, as part of its formal knowledge management process, a company should measure and publish statistics on human, social, environmental, and "integrity" performance (using international standards and reporting guidelines).

Business Research and Analysis

Finally, one of the most revolutionary and valuable features of knowledge management today is the ability for a company to gain access to enormous amounts of business research and analysis materials. As part of a KRM process, companies need to create an information-gathering capacity, developing a research and analysis capability in order to search for, organize, and distribute information from internal and external sources concerning local political, cultural, and legal concerns. This should include the ability to complete formal research in areas such as the following:

- Regulatory and legal policies
- Company violations and fines for noncompliance
- Local political, social, and regulatory climate in areas of new or potential project development
- Internet and press reports on the company's performance
- Social and environmental performance of subcontractors and their reputation in the local community
- Capturing leading practice and lessons learned (both internal and among the competition)

Community and Stakeholder Involvement

Communication and knowledge sharing is key to good knowledge management. This holds true not only for a company's employees but also for the many stakeholders who are interested in company policy. Systems such as e-mail, electronic newsletters, and collaborative online project planning can all help not only to keep stakeholders informed of company policy, but also to help company leaders sense and respond to early concerns from these stakeholders on policy matters that could later develop into serious incidents.

WHY KNOWLEDGE MANAGEMENT AND
RISK MANAGEMENT ARE COMPLEMENTARY

What is important to realize, as most readers no doubt have, is that these types of activities, and the systems, infrastructure, and processes that support them, are not so different from what many stage two companies already have in place. That is why many organizations, such as BT, Intel, or Chevron Texaco, are simply integrating and coordinating their existing safety, supply chain, and knowledge management systems in a more coordinated way, as part of a broader risk management program.

There are many benefits from actively managing the knowledge of an organization, and knowledge management has advanced far in its thinking in the past 5 years from soft to tangible practice. With a combination of new management techniques and innovative organizational and cultural practices, supported by integrated IT systems for collecting, storing, and distributing information, the active management of knowledge and information in an organization has become central to good management of the company today. Simply put, there can be no risk management without good knowledge management.

"Risk management is primarily a function of the inherent behaviors practiced by the people that make up a business," says Debra Amidon, founder and CEO of Entovation. "And it is the knowledge that these people create, use, and transfer that leads to the provision of given products or services. It therefore follows that the more effectively the organization manages this knowledge—its most precious asset—the greater the chance that business results will be favorable (i.e., that adversity is minimized and opportunities capitalized upon)."[8]

For most companies, these are the types of things—along with a stronger and more effective ethics framework, and preparations for triple–bottom-line reporting—that they should be putting in place in the next few years anyway.

Given the scandal-shaken world of business today, it only makes sense now to apply the same types of techniques that have worked so well in the quality management sphere to company-wide risk management. "Knowledge management is risk management," says Ian Martin of UBS Warburg. "It is impossible for a firm to respond to risks in the appropriate manner without having the proper knowledge in place."

"If a firm is to limit its exposure to, and the impact of, the diverse threats it encounters, it is essential that employees at every level throughout the organization are actively involved in its risk management strategy."[9]

"Ultimately," concludes Simon Lelic, "both disciplines have at their roots the values and processes that form the fundamentals of sound managerial practice, and while it may only have been the shock of recent events that has prompted companies to action, the progress such firms have made in recent months will amount to little if both KM and risk management are not, in the future, instilled in everyday operations."[10]

Finally, if all else fails and a serious incident occurs, the existence of a formal knowledge management program for identifying and dealing with legal compliance issues within a company will in itself lessen the likelihood (and magnitude) of any legal penalties.

RISK MANAGEMENT

Once a company has adopted an ethical framework and applied strong knowledge management practices, it is well on its way to behaving in a more predictable and certain way. But how can a company leverage this combination to greater effect—to use this process to actually help reduce risks to the corporation and improve performance at the same time?

The answer is that among stage three companies, that same process for collecting performance information can also be used to collect risk management information. This process now provides the opportunity for collecting key trends and information that will allow the company to anticipate, recognize, and respond to incidents and risks that can threaten the company. To understand what this process is and why it is important and different, we need to look at the fundamentals of a second discipline: risk management.

What is Risk Management?

Risk management theory is not new; it is incorporated in the very way we do business, suggested by multiple management layers and approval policies in the hierarchical organization. But, as we have seen over the past decade, many of those management layers have been removed and empowerment of employees has meant that in many companies the once burdensome approval process has been all but eliminated. At the same time, as we have seen in earlier chapters, there are new risks facing companies and new techniques and systems available for dealing with them. This combination of new threats and new opportunities makes it important now to begin to view total risk management as a strategic process in the modern company, best handled as part of a knowledge management policy.

Like knowledge management, risk management is not the best of terms, if only because management theorists have co-opted an everyday word, with all its many nuances, into the lexicon of business. And to many people, risk management is a term that has long been in use on the financial side of business. After all, risk management has its history in audit controls techniques and statistical risk calculations that are used for financial markets, for hedge funds and derivatives trading, and insurance policy calculations.

In the past decade, however, risk management has come to include a set of processes, activities, and systems that allow a company to monitor day-to-day operational threats—in terms of health and safety to employees, environmental policy, product safety, or internal ethical malfeasance—which if unnoticed and left unattended can be ruinous to a company.

In this context, risk management is the process by which a company actively screens for and reacts to potentially damaging risk incidents in a cogent way. It therefore has a natural relationship both with a company's ethical framework (in that it helps to ensure that the company senses and responds to issues in an ethical and legal way) and with the quality process, in that key information and knowledge on risk come from a combination of continuous monitoring and formal auditing. And, as we will see in Chapter 11, a strategic process of enterprise-wide risk management can be greatly enhanced by applying the standards and reporting processes that specifically focus on how a company is behaving in critical risky areas of product safety, governance, or social or environmental policy. Risk management is essentially just good management in the modern world of global business.

Risk Management Ground Rules

The value of a strategic program of risk management is best appreciated if we first begin with a few ground rules:

First, in the context in which it is used in this book, risk management has a greater practical and operational focus than in the past. Risk management is no longer just about statistical investment risk; business risk management is much more about perceiving and dealing with bad decisions or process failures and preventing those failures from damaging the company.

Second, it is important to appreciate that risk is not always bad, so risk management is not necessarily aimed at avoiding risks at all costs. After all, many discretionary decisions on product selection and marketing, advertising or investment, are very much at the heart of the business management process and need to be left to the discretion of company leadership. But many other risks exist on a day-to-day basis that can cause ruinous harm to a company simply because they are never understood, acknowledged, or dealt with in a business-like manner. In short, the key is not simply to avoid risk, but to manage risk—to recognize it, evaluate it, and deal with it—without compromising spontaneity or innovation.

Third, reflecting this shift from a financial to a strategic business focus, risk management needs to be set in the context of practical events, to take into account both fact and emotion. Managing risks well is dependent upon having accurate information and balanced views of all the factors surrounding an incident, including how other stakeholders may react. This is not something that lends itself to being done easily or systematically, because even when facts are known, decisions on the course of action to be taken are often still based on intuition and experience of employees. That is why knowledge management—leveraging the skills and expertise of your employees and collecting all necessary facts concerning the incident and stakeholder's opinion in a coherent way—is essential for good risk management.

Fourth, a risk cannot always be reduced to whether it is or is not compliant with the law. A company may pursue a policy that is perfectly within the law or at least not governed by law or regulation and yet still be doing something that can seriously damage its reputation. After all, being legally "right" is only part of the equation. One of the key principles of risk management theory is that there is more to risk than the immediate legal repercussions of the action itself, something described well by Dr. Peter Sandman in his "outrage" model. A chemical spill, for example, may only cost a company $250,000 in fines, but the real cost in terms of reputation, legal fees, share price decline, and public relations recovery effort costs would be many times that amount.

This concept of "outrage," in which public and NGO reaction continues to cause harm to the company in ways well beyond a fine or litigation costs, is very important in gauging risk. Coca-Cola suffered from this form of "outrage" in 1999 when 42 Belgian school children complained of nausea, headaches, and stomach cramps after drinking Coke. Appearing to be either indifferent or evasive, Coca-Cola executives hesitated to recall their products, explaining that "after thorough investigation, no health or safety issues were found." The next day the company did recall 2.5 million bottles from the local area, blaming defective carbon dioxide used in the bottling process. But after a total of 115 Belgian and 80 French Coca-Cola drinkers—mostly children and students—complained of similar symptoms, the Belgian, French, and Luxembourg governments ordered the removal of 65 million cans from circulation themselves. It was a stunning blow to Coca-Cola, because it was the governments, not the corporation, that had chosen to take decisive action on behalf of the public good.

Newspapers reported the company's intransigence and labeled the illness as "Coca-Colic." After a week, the Belgian Minister of Health was still contending that Coca-Cola had not provided a "a satisfactory and conclusive explanation for the symptoms" and banned the sale of all Coca-Cola drinks, urging Belgians not to drink Coca-Cola or other Coca-Cola–owned brands such as Fanta or Sprite. The Dutch, Germans, Spain, and Saudis all then followed suit.[11] Coca-Cola's CEO, Douglas Ivester, eventually made a belated statement of regret, pledging to take "all necessary steps" to guarantee the safety of its products in the future. It was a public relations disaster for the company.[12]

Types of Risk

With those ground rules in mind, it can be helpful to identify the different broad categories of risk that a company faces today.

The first type of risk is *strategic marketing risk*. In a global economy with rapidly changing technologies and market unpredictability, many companies are faced with the occasional "go for broke" decision, to create a new line of product, or to enter into a new market sector, to diversify, merge, or make a major acquisition.

With market risk, a poor decision can result in severe losses to the company or even bankruptcy, but whatever the strategic risks, these types of decisions are less likely to involve "outrage" (just pity or scorn). Analysts and investors may feel that your strategic planning was not up to much, but the incident, whatever it does to the company's reputation for product continuity, won't affect the company's reputation for probity. Customers will still buy the product if it fits in with their needs. In short, marketing risks are ingrained in management strategy, and although making the right decision can benefit from having sound information and knowledge at hand, these types of risks do not really fall under the purview of an ethical risk framework.

A second area of risk is *noncompliance with regulations or laws.* In developed economies, myriad laws govern business behavior today— environmental, employment, product safety, accounting, governance— for which violating or ignoring can lead to fines, legal costs, and often damage to a company's reputation. These are the types of violations that cause "outrage" and are governed by specific legal codes and guidelines, such as generally accepted accounting practices, Occupational Safety and Health Administration (OSHA), environmental health and safety, or equal opportunity employment (EOE) laws.

Most companies have at least a fair understanding of these rules and have specialists from legal, human resources, or finance who monitor company policy to ensure compliance. For manufacturing, product, and environmental safety, this is all part of what most companies call "process safety management" (PSM). What is alarming, though, is that despite PSM, and despite rigorous Environmental Protection Agency (EPA), OSHA, and EOE standards and monitoring, companies still continue, every day, to violate these regulations. Included among these violations are issues concerning product safety, defrauding customers, environmentally illegal practices, or employment or civil rights law violations that we have been examining in earlier chapters.

A third form of risk comes from "discretionary issues." This is a hybrid category of risks that may not be governed by laws or regulations yet can easily cause outrage among pressure groups, the media, or the public. These types of risk issues involve judgments about issues that may not be obviously illegal but can have a disastrous effect on the corporate reputation.

Coca-Cola's problems with contaminated products in Belgium are a good example of a poorly managed discretionary issue. Similarly,

LookSmart, the Web search engine, was the subject of a class-action suit alleging breach of contract when in 2002 it fundamentally shifted its business strategy from a one-time charge to marketers to be placed as a directory listing in its search results to a pay-per-click system in which marketers paid a transaction fee per hit on its site. It was in fact simply following a trend for collecting fees that is moving through the industry, but it enraged its subscribers.

There may well be, as in this example, a legal argument against the company (breach of contract), but what really alienated—outraged—LookSmart clients was the perceived deception.

"The biggest complaint was that LookSmart did this without any warning," said Chris Sherman, associate editor of industry newsletter SearchEngineWatch.com. "The perception in the Web-master community is that LookSmart didn't handle it very well, and the class-action lawsuit reflects that."

Whatever the results of the legal suit, 1 month after the policy the company had signed up only 8000 companies for its small-business listings, about one tenth of the former 90,000 subscribers for the service.[13]

Discretionary policies—deciding what your company should do in terms of reacting to a crisis, setting up in a dangerous or politically volatile labor market, or responding to accusations by a pressure group—tend to require a much more nuanced decision-making process than simple issues of compliance. It may not be apparent at the time which particular policy or response will be most effective in avoiding a crisis or indeed whether any response is needed.

Peter Sandman refers to this as "yellow flag" territory. These are the kinds of issues that are neither obviously trivial (green flag) nor obviously dangerous and require immediate remedy (red flag). Yellow flags fall into this middle ground, and it is here that many organizations find themselves poorly prepared to respond strategically. Navigating through these yellow-flag situations can be one of the most difficult management challenges in modern business.

And yet, because these types of issues can often lead to serious "outrage," the more that is known about a product or a policy's impact and the likely reaction by stakeholders, the better. Therefore, one of the first decisions that must be made when facing a yellow-flag situation is how to react to the potential problem as it stands and what other information corporate decision makers need in order to make a policy decision. That is why, as we will see, mobilizing the knowledge of employees with subject expertise becomes so important to a program of risk management.

As with compliance-based issues, the first and most important step is usually appreciating the fact that a potential problem exists at all. For that reason, discretionary issues still call for the same sort of knowledge management discovery process as any other potentially damaging compliance issue. Unfortunately, companies seldom have in place the necessary combination of early warning systems, experts, and evidence necessary for making an informed decision in these difficult and dangerous scenarios.

Once again, this brings us back to the thesis of this book: that a company needs to actively manage risk based upon a formal ethical framework, accepted international guidelines, KRM techniques, and an honest and transparent reporting system.

WHY GOOD COMPANIES DO REALLY BAD THINGS . . .

Fundamentally, there are three reasons why unethical or illegal activities occur in an otherwise law-abiding and ethical company:

First, and by far the most common reason, the executives and corporate organizational leaders simply don't know what is happening. "Almost without exception," says Jim Kartalia, president of Entegra, "crisis postmortems show that the primary reason trivial incidents mushroom into devastating scandals is that the events were not reported soon enough or at a high enough level."[14]

Second, executives do know that a potential problem exists, and once that potential is discovered, they attempt to remedy the situation as required by law, with no sense of how their response itself can be potentially damaging to the company's reputation. In short, they move toward compliance, ignoring the potential dangers of "outrage."

Third, and most devastating, company leaders do know what is happening, realize the possible ethical or legal repercussions, but mistakenly think it is worth risking anyway, assuming that either they are unlikely to be caught or the damage is unlikely to take them outside the threshold of their company's acceptable level of risk tolerance. All three of these scenarios reflect failures of knowledge and risk management.

Reputation Management

Finally, I should also say a word about reputation management. With risk and reputation so integrally intertwined, *reputation management* is a term often used synonymously with *risk management,* although in fact it is probably more appropriately thought of as a subset of risk management.

Risk management helps a corporation to avoid disasters that may cost the company lost sales, a decrease in share value, fines. or legal restrictions. *Reputation management* is a term that is now used to describe the process by which a firm constantly analyzes its image in terms of views held by its various stakeholders, including customers, investors, analysts, pressure groups, unions, and the media. It is essentially an ongoing scan of those interest groups, usually done by an outside firm, that takes periodic samples of how your company is perceived by those groups.

This type of reputation sampling has been buoyed by recent press and business management suggestions that a company's reputation can be leveraged—through brand marketing or "cause-related marketing"—and that an organization's reputation is therefore one of its most strategic assets. A recent survey by risk and insurance groups completed by Lloyd's of London, for example, found that 62 percent of those professionals thought loss of reputation was the most significant risk facing businesses today.[15] *CEO Magazine* in the United States, in surveying the opinions of chief executives, found a similar result, with 95 percent of CEOs listing "reputation" as one of the most critical aspects of continued success.

It is a legitimate consideration and can be an effective marketing tool. Unfortunately, despite the integral appreciation for the need to maintain a good brand image, reputation management for the most part deals less with avoiding problems that might destroy a company's brand reputation, as it does monitoring perceptions and enhancing an organization's image. It generally takes two forms.

The first form of reputation management is little more than what is often known as a "clipping service," which involves straightforward image research based on media scans. The more sophisticated consulting firms not only help a company to monitor and understand how the outside world perceives it but also provide a service that helps a company to understand whether its advertising and public relations messages are getting through. Often sold as part of an early warning system for identifying risks to a company's reputation, these types of media scans can be a valuable tool for marketing but are generally very much removed from serious risk management.

The second form of reputation management is a more comprehensive type of survey mechanism, referred to by the larger audit groups such as PricewaterhouseCoopers as "reputation assurance." This service analyzes what risks the company might be likely to face but concentrates more on how various stakeholders view the corporation, its products, and overall image. These may involve more complex studies that reveal how a corporation is perceived by financial analysts and banks before applying for access to capital or the likelihood of approval for a "license to operate" in particular communities where the corporation is contemplating entering. These services often include a broad set of customer surveys, public opinion polls, and other survey tools.

There are many good examples. Infonic, a consultancy based in London, for example, provide "brand-monitoring" services that address such questions as the following:

- Which of the issues your business faces are growing in intensity?
- Who are the key online opinion formers?
- How do issues move between audiences?
- Which NGOs lead the debate, and what is their stance and their strategies?[16]

Ultimately, the goal of these groups is to incorporate an appreciation for the need to maintain a good reputation into the major processes of a company, including marketing, plant operations, quality, strategic planning, and product development. The advantages to this type of service is that it takes into account a broad sampling of stakeholders, and the information can be a valuable tool when used as part of a company's broader risk management program.

A second group of companies offer a related service, almost entirely based on a public relations solution. This service, in fact, has become one of the main offerings of public relations firms these days. These groups analyze a company's current reputation through stakeholder and Internet scanning, and then provide recommendations on how to improve on that reputation through public relations techniques such as lobbying for positions on a "most admired company" list or getting positive coverage in the media for philanthropic efforts. Although effective at times, these types of public relations–based attempts at reputation manipulation can have their drawbacks, with pressure groups citing the cynical and manipulative nature of this type of approach. In fact, it is just this type of public relations focus that has led to accusations by activists and the media of general corporate insincerity—of "greenwash"—when it comes to ethical behavior and corporate social responsibility.

CHAPTER ENDNOTES

[1] Gary Abramson. "Consultants Clamor for Companies' Attention and KM Dollars," *CIO Enterprise Magazine,* May 15, 1999. Available from www.cio.com/archive/enterprise/051599_cons_content.html.

2 Simon Lelic, "Managing Knowledge to Manage Risk," *Knowledge Management* 6, no. 1 (September 2, 2002). Available from www.kmmagazine.com.

3 Simon Lelic, "Managing Knowledge to Manage Risk," *Knowledge Management* 6, no. 1 (September 2, 2002). Available from www.kmmagazine.com.

4 Peter Marsh, "Shared Knowledge Lifts Margins," *Financial Times,* July 2, 2002.

5 Simon Lelic, "Managing Knowledge to Manage Risk," *Knowledge Management* 6, no. 1 (September 2, 2002). Available from www.kmmagazine.com.

6 Simon Lelic, "Managing Knowledge to Manage Risk." *Knowledge Management* 6, 1 (September 2, 2002). Available from www.kmmagazine.com.

7 Dave Stangis, interview with the author, January 23, 2003.

8 Simon Lelic, "Managing Knowledge to Manage Risk," *Knowledge Management* 6, no. 1 (September 2, 2002). Available from www.kmmagazine.com.

9 Simon Lelic, "Managing Knowledge to Manage Risk," *Knowledge Management* 6, no. 1 (September 2, 2002). Available from www.kmmagazine.com.

10 Simon Lelic, "Managing Knowledge to Manage Risk," *Knowledge Management* 6, no. 1 (September 2, 2002). Available from www.kmmagazine.com.

11 James Graff, "Big Fizzle for Coca-Cola," *Time Magazine,* June 28, 1999. Available from www.time.com/time/magazine/intl/article/0,9171,1107990628–27849,00.html.

12 "Coca-Cola 'Regrets' Contamination," *BBC News Online,* June 17, 1999. Available from news.bbc.co.uk/2/hi/europe/371300.stm.

13 Stefanie Olsen, "LookSmart Fees Backfire into Lawsuit." News.com Web site, June 4, 2002. Available from news.com.com/2100–1023–932032.html.

14 Jim Kartalia, "Reputation at Risk," *Risk Management,* May 2000.

15 Jim Kartalia, "Reputation at Risk," *Risk Management,* May 2000.

16 Infonic Web site, www.infonic.com.

EIGHT

Integrating Ethics, Risk, Standards, and Knowledge Management into an Ethical Framework

Although most corporations have developed some aspects of each of the key areas that we have been talking about, a single broad process for avoiding corporate disasters, certainly for most stage one and stage two companies, has remained largely "unmanaged." However, as the outside world begins to exert greater pressures on corporations to behave well—through aggressive mass media, pressure groups, legislation, regulation, and litigation—progressive companies are realizing just how imperative and strategically important it is that they develop and coordinate these four key areas, in order to avoid foolish and costly ethical or legal blunders.

Of course no company will be able to protect itself against all types of risks. The very nature of decision making and discretion means that organizations will still make catastrophically bad decisions from time to time on discretionary issues regarding such areas as product marketing, advertising, or public relations. However, at the very least, these decisions should be made based on a clear understanding of the issues, on the opinion of important stakeholders, and on the likely repercussions to the organization.

More importantly, corporations can go a long way toward preventing the compliance-based violations that can ruin a reputation and cost the company millions, and that usually come about through unintentional actions or because executives are never made aware of the problems. To do that, a company must identify likely risks before they occur, assess their exposure, and then take logical steps to eliminate the risk and to mitigate damage, a type of decision-making process that is dependent upon an integrated approach to ethics and risk management.

There is no single model for integrating knowledge and risk management (KRM) that can be applied across the board to companies large and small, in various industries. Methods vary widely among stage three and four companies. Intel, for example, uses a formal process for collecting risk information from its customer service agents and customer resource management (CRM) system and from its ongoing environmental health and safety (EHS) approach, its environmental management systems, and its 14001 certification process. McDonald's provides employees with a point-and-click incident management system that is available in every restaurant so employees can enter any incidents immediately and confidentially, to be recorded and acted on in a formal incident management process.

Other companies have a more formal ongoing process such as the ones we describe later in this chapter. No matter which approach your company may choose, there are two important principles to keep in mind:

- The process should be formally managed.
- It should involve employees from the shop floor to the executives.

A PROGRAM OF INTEGRATED KNOWLEDGE AND RISK MANAGEMENT

One organizational concept that has proven valuable over the past 10 years is that the more a company can integrate its different functional silos, in terms of process, systems, and communications, the more productive and effective the organization will be. This was the logic behind the business process reengineering movement of the early 1990s and has increasingly become the commanding theory of efficiency, incorporated in new Enterprise Resource Planning (ERP) platforms, Enterprise Application Integration activities, and with new extended supply chain practices. In addition, as we have seen, it is this same enterprise-wide coordinating effect that has been the basis for the development of the knowledge management movement. As we are beginning to understand, it is the evolutionary nature of efficiency in a company to integrate and coordinate.

The same is true of risk management. After all, as we have seen, risk to a company can come about because of, or at least involve, many different groups in an organization: operational health and safety, human resources, technology, finance and accounting, strategic planning, and public relations. It is unworkable for an organization to try to manage risk on a departmental or functional basis when ultimately the result will have an impact on other functions and on the reputation of the firm overall. For this reason, the next imperative for corporations is to provide an integrated, coordinated management process that manages risk throughout the organization using leading KRM techniques and enterprise systems.

"Integrated risk management," notes the Treasury Board of Canada in its "Best Practices in Risk Management" report, "is a continuous, proactive, and systematic process to understand, manage, and communicate risk from an organization-wide perspective."[1] (It, like several other federal, state, and local authorities in Canada, Britain, and Australia, has advocated this type of integrated risk management approach for local government.)

At an organizational level, the goal of this integrated enterprise-wide risk management process is to allow a company to actively scan for potential risks that confront the organization at all levels, in all departments, allowing company experts and decision makers to analyze and prioritize those risks and manage them at a corporate level.

As in all stage three and four companies, the process should be as follows:

- Systematically applied: Not left to develop in a piecemeal, haphazard, or unmanaged way.
- Consistent and continuous: The process cannot simply be put in effect once a problem has come about; it should be integrated into the DNA of business strategy, planning, operations, and day-to-day decision making.
- Proactive: No matter what types of risk your organization faces, it pays to have these types of processes in place before things go wrong. That means developing ground rules, formally establishing a system for identifying and escalating issues, and putting in place procedures and resources that are trained to react to those issues.

Key Phases of a Program of Integrated Risk Management

There are many ways to approach an integrated process of KRM, but one way is simply to break down the process into 11 generic steps:

- Planning the KRM framework
- Building a dedicated ethics and risk management team
- Completing an initial risk "scan" to identify and prioritize major company risk areas and to test the readiness of the company to react to potential incidents
- Identifying key experts through knowledge mapping and "hard tagging"
- Creating an "accountability matrix" of key decision makers and process owners
- Identifying and training "early alert" teams
- Incorporating key techniques into existing operational and management structures
- Educating and training employees at all levels
- Reacting to a risk situation

- Creating an executive risk review matrix
- Monitoring, reevaluating, and "adjusting"

Step One: Planning the Knowledge and Risk Management Framework

Preparatory work will require the active support of senior executives, dedicated resource, time, money, considerable planning, and a good deal of diplomacy and communication. For that reason, the first step for companies that are ready to move toward an integrated risk management approach is to develop the business case and enlist executive and board support. Key steps should include building a case for action, taking that case to corporate leaders and board members for sponsorship and endorsement, and getting the necessary funding and resources approved.

Step Two: Building the Ethics and Knowledge and Risk Management Team

As we have noted before, although the chief executive officer and the board of directors should be directly involved in the risk management process, many companies that have developed a strong risk management framework have an internal risk management group, headed by the chief ethics officer in a what is often a combined role—chief ethics and risk officer (CERO)—with assistance from a dedicated team of risk facilitators.

This specialist risk management group, like the knowledge coordinators of knowledge management projects, is responsible for the success of the overall program, as well as for communicating the goals, principles and procedures to employees, and acting as a center of excellence for consultation on all matters of ethics and risk. These activities include the following:

- Communicating the business case for action for a risk management process to all employees

- Facilitating educational and early risk scanning workshops
- Providing advice and continuity
- Collecting, assessing, and prioritizing risks that are identified throughout the company
- Preparing the risk matrix for senior management
- Monitoring compliance
- Emergency reporting of serious risks

Facilitators are important initially because they can help communicate the need and the method for the initial risk scan (see the next section) and bring some continuity to the process for identifying risks at the grassroots business level. In a large corporation, these facilitators will attend hundreds of small group meetings, explaining the process and the business case, and encouraging employees to help identify risks on a daily basis. As this process of risk scanning becomes more routine, the role of the facilitators largely disappears, and line managers themselves become responsible for escalating potential risks back to the CERO. Facilitators usually become part of the Ethics and Risk Committee and continue in a liaison and education role, although no longer actively facilitating meetings.

Finally, because many of these activities have traditionally been the responsibility of a company's Internal Audit Committee, members from that committee may be co-opted or form the bulk of the resources of this group. Equally important, the chief knowledge officer (if the company has one) and representation from MIS (information technology) should be integrally involved with the design and planning stage.

Dave Stangis, Intel's manager for corporate responsibility, explains that Intel has a "virtual network" of interested directors who meet on a quarterly basis to discuss process links and collaboration in terms of key risk issues. Many managers—from its risk management group, EHS, legal, emerging issues management, or corporate affairs—have a similar interest in key issues. "A part of each of their job is focused on corporate reputation and corporate responsibility and other risk management issues—there are pieces in there in terms of legal liabilities, health and safety, facility safety, compliance and so forth, that crossover roles—so we talk as a team."[2]

Step Three: Completing an Initial Risk "Scan" and Corporate-Readiness Assessment

Step three involves understanding the likely areas of risk exposure facing your organization and determining how well the company is currently prepared to detect, preempt, or resolve a serious incident. This means first looking at the company's core activities—product development, health and safety, environmental policy, employment policies—and determining where potential risks are most likely to occur. This initial assessment can best be done through a risk analysis process, sometimes known as a risk "scan."

This process is a repeatable method for scanning for risks that once the basic approach is understood can be done on an almost daily basis in order to sense and respond to potential or emerging risks around the company. There are two components of risk scanning.

The first component is an *initial corporate risk readiness assessment*, which examines how well the company is prepared to recognize and react to potential risks. This is conducted at the outset of the project and is integral both to creating a case for action and for beginning the employee education and training process.

Usually conducted by members of the company's Ethics Committee and overseen by the chief ethics officer, this initial risk scan usually consists of a series of facilitated information-gathering workshops and training sessions at various levels throughout the organization.

The second component *ongoing risk scanning* is begun with this initial corporate-sponsored program but then continues on a regular basis as line managers pick up responsibility for continuing the risk-scanning process on an ongoing basis, by incorporating a risk analysis for their area into regular employee and management meetings. This process for ongoing issue scanning—the basis for collecting issues and concerns from line employees—begins to incorporate the risk management process directly into day-to-day operations at all levels of the company.

The Initial Risk Scan

An initial scan needs to identify and focus at a minimum on key areas where risky behavior is likely to occur, for example, the launch of a new or controversial product, a new project, or a reoccurring or potentially dangerous manufacturing or support activity. It should also focus on the key areas that we looked at earlier in this book, such as regulatory compliance, EHS, equal opportunity employment compliance, and aspects of corporate governance. Other issues might include risks involving the following:

- Retail site selection
- Local employment
- Living-wage policies
- Layoffs and downsizing policies
- Adherence to local "cultural norms" in foreign economies
- Union membership
- Security
- Employee privacy

There are many different types of tools or methods—many learned from knowledge management techniques—for this type of risk scanning. These include straightforward interviews, brainstorming workshops with employees or stakeholders, "what if" scenario reviews, or confidential opinion polls and surveys. This process should also involve various stakeholders such as unions, nongovernmental organizations (NGOs), regulatory agencies, and local community leaders.

Rather than have members of the Ethics Committee (now ominously often called an Ethics and Risk [E/R] Committee) complete this initial risk assessment alone, some organizations have their E/R

Committee coaches simply provide first-level managers with a collection of templates, checklists, and leading practice guidelines, prompting them to work with their immediate reporting employees to analyze potential issues and evaluate risk themselves. Once identified and prioritized, these operational managers themselves then take issues that they have registered as important up the managerial ladder.

The obvious advantages of this method are that it makes managers themselves responsible for day-to-day risk management from the outset of the project and it is a less formal and less employee–intensive process. The obvious problem with this approach is that managers may not want information that possibly reflects badly on their performance to move up the corporate ladder and often do not appreciate the wider, strategic consequences of local issues. That is where the E/R Committee coaches become invaluable.

There are many ways of analyzing company risk during this initial assessment, including surveys, confidential questionnaires, and group workshops. For specific operational risks, many companies are already using some form of HAZOP study, which is a methodology, usually with accompanying software, for identifying operational hazards. Most production or manufacturing companies will already have experience with these types of reviews as part of their process safety management (PSM) practices, usually required by the Environmental Protection Agency (EPA) or the Occupational Safety and Health Administration (OSHA).

There are other more complex methods for technical diagnosis of risks such as fault-tree or effects analysis, but these are seldom helpful at this level of risk scanning, where the main goal is to simply identify the key areas of potential concern and understand how well the company is prepared to react to an incident.

One of the first results of the scan should be to reveal areas, usually widely recognized but seldom formally spoken about, in the operational work environment that are knowingly violating ethical or compliance rules. In this regard, questions need to focus on routing out problem areas such as a prevailing culture either in the corporation as a whole or in specific departments that finds "fudging" of ethical or legal guidelines acceptable. If there have been frequent EHS violations, for example, how have local managers, as well as senior corporate leaders, responded?

This risk-scanning process has both a proactive and a reactive component. The initial purpose is to identify, proactively, broad areas or activities in which risks are likely to occur. However, the initial scan, which reveals a "snapshot" of the corporation's current risk situation can be repeated once every quarter or twice yearly to continually monitor the company's risk situation and the progress of managers and groups. This should still be completed by the E/R Committee.

The Ongoing Risk-Scanning Process

The process of ongoing risk management should gradually become the responsibility of employees and managers throughout the organization, built into the operational processes of the company through a formal process that encourages risk discussion and assessment in all operational meetings and activities.

As the process matures, this ongoing risk-scanning process (combined with quarterly or biyearly audits performed by the E/R Committee) encourages employees at all levels to actively anticipate potential problem areas and activities that are most likely to present a threatening incident of safety, regulatory violation, or indiscretion.

Again, Intel serves as a good example. "One of the things that helps us," says Dave Stangis, "is that our environmental, health, and safety organization continues to strive to be out in front—especially in terms of learning from repeat or near-miss kinds of things. They have whole networks of information around the globe—we call it the "EHS workstations"—that track every single incident, digs into root causes, and puts in place actions so it doesn't happen again."

"These things," he explains, "are all reported quarterly to the senior management. It has been that way for a decade, so it is a really robust system. . . . So now we are looking at new ways to go beyond simply learning from mistakes and are now trying to anticipate potential issues."[3]

Just as there is a division between ethical and operational risks, the scanning process also needs to take into account risks that occur at both the corporate and the operational level. At the corporate level, incidents will be more strategic in nature, and should include political, economic, and social issues relating to planned new investments. Typical corporate-level issues might include examining proposed projects and how they may affect and be received by the local communities, either domestically or in developing nations. Similarly, a strategic risk scan should examine likely environmental or social issues associated with the proposed project in a risky market, such as issues of bribery, official corruption, health, or political turmoil.

Assessing these types of risk seems an obvious part of making strategic decisions, yet it is surprising how seldom these issues are analyzed in a coherent way, using the knowledge and expertise of nonexecutive employees. Nor are concerns always brought to the attention of other organizational leaders until after key strategic and operational decisions have been made, money allocated, and NGO denunciations already making headlines.

The process must not just be internally focused. It also should identify the broad spectrum of stakeholders who may be affected by a project, a product, or a plant relocation. In this regard, integral to this ongoing risk-scanning process should be contact in a formal and consistent way with key stakeholders (e.g., unions, local community leaders, NGOs and pressure groups, government officials, suppliers, and business partners) that have a direct interest or influence over the company's reputation.

It is important to remember that this risk-scanning process is neither an employee satisfaction survey nor (from other stakeholders) just a reputation scan. Once established, it should be seen as a continuous ongoing search for issues at all levels of the organization. The objective is to discover potential problem areas and to quickly begin to understand the company's options should an incident occur. That is why the entire process must be fully integrated into current processes, structures, and systems. Long-term trends are important, but these types of scans occasionally will highlight a more immediate urgent concern that might have been overlooked or suppressed if a formal process were not in place.

The end result of this initial risk scan is to build a readiness profile that can be brought to senior management and the board as a basis for recommendations as a part of confirming a business case for moving ahead with an integrated risk management process. Based on this readiness profile, a company can move forward and begin to identify resources and assign roles and responsibilities.

Step Four: Identifying Key Experts through Knowledge Mapping and "Hard Tagging"

As we have seen, formally identifying and "hard tagging" company and external specialists is a key tenet of knowledge management.

At Intel, for example, the development of these communities of practice, or "virtual networks," is key to their enterprise-wide risk management process. "What we are trying to do," says Dave Stangis, "is to better institutionalize all of these great virtual networks that we have. And a lot of that, I admit, is still 'people glue' and individual knowledge and energy linked up, all wanting to do the right thing. There are people in almost every organization at Intel who really find energy and personal interest in this corporate responsibility, or what ever name you choose to call it, doing the right thing . . . and they drive a lot of this."[4]

Step Five: Creating an "Accountability Matrix" of Key Decision Makers and Process Owners

It is important to determine who the key decision makers will be during a crisis so they, along with other experts, are aware and well informed about an incident from the outset. As Patrick Caragata, author of *Risk: The Invisible Killer* notes, "Especially for small companies with smaller staff, you need to identify the people who you can turn to in a crisis long before the crisis begins."[5]

Step Six: Identifying and Training "Early Alert" Teams

Once a risk arises, either through the scanning process or from the continuous risk process now incorporated in day-to-day management meetings and morning reviews, a company needs to determine how to react. Having set up procedures for identifying risks it is now important to bring together the necessary resources for analyzing, assessing and prioritizing them.

Once a risk is raised, depending on its nature and perceived urgency, the CERO convenes an "early alert" team (sometimes known as an incident or crisis management team), which at the discretion of the CERO can consist, as necessary, of the following:

- Employees who understand the immediate circumstances of the situation
- Managers in the command chain up to the chief executive officer (CEO)
- Legal and human resources representatives
- A representative from the company's "internal audit" group
- "Hard-tagged" specialists who have relevant experience with similar incidents
- A representative from Corporate Affairs

This early alert team forms the core group with responsibility for assessing the risk and reporting to the E/R Committee. They are usually supported by electronic systems (see Chapter 10) as appropriate, for example, an incident management or risk management system, related knowledge databases for legal and personnel issues, and e-mail groupware for communicating, distributing relevant documentation, and scheduling meetings. For advanced companies that have a knowledge management regime in place, a database of similar issues in the past may be available for comparison and lessons learned, along with the names of employees who can be contacted who were involved in resolving earlier similar incidents.

Step Seven: Incorporating Key Techniques into Existing Operational and Management Structures

Once the initial risk scanning is complete, the same scanning process should be incorporated directly into the company's operational framework. This is usually most effectively done simply by making regular risk reviews part of all employee and management meetings. Although alternatives to the continuous risk scanning should always be available (e.g., confidential e-mail or hot-line contacts), it is important not to allow this process to be seen as bureaucratic or separate from the company's existing operational, management, and decision-making structures. On a regular basis, employees should be asked as part of a formal process what if any possible risks they perceive might be arising in their area.

Most companies find that tools such as surveys or formal brainstorming, though occasionally justified and useful during the initial scan, quickly contribute to "survey fatigue" and a perception among employees that the risk management process is still essentially audit based and separate from their day-to-day responsibilities. One of the most effective methods for revealing possible risks is for managers to simply throw out the following question during their regular employee meetings: "Is there anything we are doing that may result in an incident that will damage the reputation of the company?" By simply incorporating regular risk management analysis into everyday meetings, reports, and existing roles, a company not only keeps costs down but also "normalizes" the process.

"Managers should be conscious of risk management and integrate it into their other management practices," advises the Treasury Board of Canada. "Overly bureaucratic and complex processes will submerge risk management into irrelevance. Managers need the flexibility to use techniques that make sense for them and their operation. However, the technique must allow for the roll up and comparison of operating unit results at the corporate level."[6]

The environmental scan has the advantage of raising both potential and immediate risks. For those risks that are identified in the process as serious, the committee will already be monitoring events and the board and CEO will be actively involved until they are resolved.

Ongoing Risk Monitoring and Reporting

The vast majority of issues that are raised during an ongoing environmental risk-scanning process are usually quickly resolved by first-level management. After all, most risks are best identified and dealt with by functional managers on the shop floor, salespeople dealing directly with distributors, or procurement staff that work with suppliers on a daily basis. Nonetheless, as a part of an ongoing process of documentation and monitoring, these identified risks, as well as a log of actions taken and a summary of the risk's resolution, need to be captured in formal incident reports.

To motivate employees to contribute something worthwhile to this ongoing risk-scanning process, risk identification must become part of the way business is done every day. This means not only that risk management needs to be part of daily meetings and the ongoing operational decision-making process but participation has to be part of employees' performance evaluation and incentive program (see Chapter 9). Building an ongoing report of those activities to be reviewed by the E/R Committee as part of a manager's compensation package is a strong motivation for taking the program seriously.

There are several ways that this information can become part of your company's reporting system, but a cascading of reports upward usually seems to be the easiest and most effective method. Key issues are raised as part of the "executive risk review matrix" presented to the CEO and the board usually on a weekly basis.

For a more general monitoring of risks and the progress of the risk process itself, some organizations have individual process and functional managers who report three or four times a year to the Ethics Committee itself, highlighting what risks have surfaced and detailing their actions to help control them. The Risk Management Committee in turn produces an internal report (usually quarterly or biannually) that is presented to the CEO and the board-level Ethics Committee, explaining the key areas of risk that were identified through the environmental scan and detailing the actions that are being taken to mitigate those risks. These reports in turn, with the most progressive companies, become part of their triple–bottom-line reporting process.

Marks and Spencer, the UK retailer, for example, has each of its group businesses regularly assess risk—financial, ethical, social, and environmental—according to likelihood and severity. These risk assessments are then sent to the company's corporate governance department that then presents the information to the Group Operating Committee, which is chaired by the CEO and includes representatives from the board, audit, and CSR committees. Roger Holmes, the chief executive, then presents the company's "risk profile" to the corporate board twice a year.[7]

Benefits of the Risk-Scanning Process

Of course, the risk-scanning process is more than just the best method for identifying and dealing with potential issues that can cause the company harm. The very fact that the process is formal and ongoing and involves many levels of the organization stresses to employees throughout the company the value placed on ethical behavior and risk awareness.

The process also helps in a more long-term way. After all, one of the most effective practices developed in the knowledge management process is to create a risk "knowledge base" of issues that have arisen in the past and lessons that have been learned from their resolution.

"Corporations need to build a reputation risk knowledge base of issues, incidents, and problems, as well as the outcomes, results, and solutions," contends Jim Kartalia. "Historical information about incidents, combined with the information gained from the identification process, provides management with a powerful and complete knowledge database to help build better training and more successful prevention programs."[8]

It is only through this type of historical information that executives can assess how well the risk management program is working and make adjustments as necessary. It also helps to provide a business case over the long term for doubters.

Moreover, given what seems to be an inexorable movement by companies globally to move toward triple–bottom-line reporting, these types of historical knowledge repositories are going to be required more and more of companies as part of that reporting process. There can be little doubt that in the unlikely event that a corporate disaster does occur, despite a strong risk management program, executives and board members will have a much stronger position to defend their actions, if they have a complete and accurate account of all actions taken. It is the only way to prove to outside auditors and potential litigants that the company leadership had done all it possibly could to avoid unethical or illegal behavior.

Possibly most important of all, this type of reporting also demonstrates that the company values a knowledge-sharing culture, and that as a company it learns and improves continuously. After all, the knowledge-sharing culture, more than even the risk management process itself, is what will help a company identify and deal with risks and unethical behavior. It is the type of process that demonstrates best that employee openness and opinions are valued, and that the company encourages information and knowledge sharing and supports those employees who value a strong ethical culture.

It also promotes many of the most important aspects of knowledge management itself: collecting lessons learned through learning audits and after-event reviews, sharing best practices, tapping into the experience and opinion of employees at all levels, respecting the value of the opinions of stakeholders, and building continuous learning plans into not only the risk management process but also the day-to-day operations and decision-making processes.

Step Eight: Educating and Training Employees at All Levels

Employees need clear and detailed guidance on what they need to do when risk or ethical issues arise in the workplace. Accordingly, a strong program of ethical and risk management education and training is essential to gaining "buy-in" from employees at all levels. As we will see in Chapter 9, this education and training program is an important first step toward developing a knowledge-sharing culture and should combine both theoretical and practical aspects of ethics and risk management.

Step Nine: Reacting to an Identified Risk

Once a potential risk has been identified, the CERO and his or her "early alert team" needs to analyze, categorize, and prioritize the risk (Figure 8.1).

Initially the team will want to rank the risk in terms of several key factors. The first factor is the *effect of the risk on the company and stakeholders.* This should be discussed in terms of best- and worst-case scenarios, listing who might be affected, and in what way, for example, reputation, property, employee morale, possible litigation, fines, or NGO outrage.

It is also important to *consider the company's ability to control the risk.* In some scenarios, such as a hurricane or natural disaster, the company may have little actual preventive control but will want to consider disaster preparedness, backup systems, and evacuation policies. In other scenarios, such as repeated EPA violations, a possible safety issue, or employment of underage workers in a developing country, the company is likely to have a high degree of control over the issue, whatever the relative costs.

Impact	Risk Management Actions		
Significant	Considerable management required	Must manage and monitor risks	Extensive management essential
Moderate	Risks may be worth accepting with monitoring	Management effort worthwhile	Management effort required
Minor	Accept risks	Accept, but monitor risks	Manage and monitor risks
	Low	Medium **Likelihood**	High

FIGURE 8.1   *The Way That the Treasury Board of Canada Looks at a Risk Assessment Model*

Another factor to consider is the *likelihood that the risk will materialize.* This is usually going to be based only on the best judgment of the team members, but that is why it is so important that a cross-functional team, experienced with facing and resolving similar incidents in the past, is formally mobilized.

Many of these rankings are highly subjective, but ranking will become more obvious the better the team understands the issue and its potential effect on various stakeholders. Every organization has different levels of risk tolerance, and that needs to be considered in this process. However, as we noted earlier, only discretionary risks should be considered part of this type of assessment process. Compliance-related risks should be dealt with in absolute and immediate terms. Too often, stage one or stage two companies have felt that they were willing to take a chance and suffer the consequences on compliance-related issues, but this undermines the entire ethical process, from values through the ethical code, and ultimately, risks outrage not only by stakeholders but serious damage to the company's reputation and to employee morale. As part of their adherence to company values, executives and company leaders need to repeat as if a mantra, "It is unethical, and illegal, it is not what our company is about, and it is never worth the risk."

In addition, of course, even discretionary risks (i.e., those that do not involve legal compliance) need to be assessed with the "outrage" factor (discussed in Chapter 7) in mind. Yet, as we have seen with the many examples throughout this book, too often this type of decision is made without really analyzing what those consequences, in terms of reputation and "outrage," might have on the company.

That is why, once again, a formal risk management approach is best used in combination with a strong and well-established ethical framework. It is only when responsible decision makers can refer back to these company values, the code of conduct, and the guidelines established under their reporting initiatives, that they can make a decision on risk based upon that context.

The combination of an ethics framework, strong standards, and a formal risk-review process means that stage three and stage four companies will have a much lower tolerance for environmental, employment, health, or safety risks, and possibly a greater tolerance and more realistic appreciation of perceived risks when it comes to marketing or product development.

Step Ten: Create a Risk Matrix for Senior Management

As with any good executive-level report, it is important to be able to extract information from several sources (e.g., quality reports, the risk scan, and EHS compliance audits) and to summarize, often on a single page, the various major risks that a company faces in both the immediate and the longer term. This is particularly valuable when repeated EHS violations are occurring, which independently and at a department level may never have been recognized as a concern by senior management.

This type of analysis is not only important for anticipating upcoming risks but also can help senior management and the board to understand patterns of behavior, trends, or the interrelationship of risks that could potentially develop into incidents.

Step Eleven: Monitor, Reevaluate, and "Adjust"/Review, Learn, and Record

Finally, it is important that employees continuously learn from the process, incorporating lessons learned into new procedures and conveying those lessons to other employees through education, training, and the communication program.

CHAPTER ENDNOTES

[1] "Best Practices in Risk Management: Public and Private Sectors Internationally," Treasury Board of Canada Web site. Available from www.tbs-sct.gc.ca/pubs_pol/dcgpubs/riskmanagement/rm-pps2_e.html#_toc456660351.

[2] Dave Stangis, interviewed by the author, January 23, 2003.

[3] Dave Stangis, interviewed by the author, January 23, 2003.

[4] Dave Stangis, interviewed by the author, January 23, 2003.

[5] Kali Pearson, "Risk: The Invisible Killer," Profitguide.com, February 3, 2003. Available from www.profitguide.com.

[6] "Best Practices in Risk Management: Public and Private Sectors Internationally," Treasury Board of Canada Web site. Available from www.tbs-sct.gc.ca/pubs_pol/dcgpubs/riskmanagement/rm-pps2_e.html#_toc456660351.

[7] Alison Maitland, "The Value of a Good Reputation," *Financial Times*, March 30, 2003.

[8] Jim Kartalia, "Reputation at Risk?" *Risk Management*, May 2000. Available from www.rims.org/mmag.

NINE

Creating a Culture of Integrity and Knowledge Sharing

Creating a culture that values and guards a company's integrity is not something that can be done instantly and depends upon being able to coordinate employee knowledge and efficient information-gathering and analysis techniques, with decision-support systems, ethical guidelines, and strong and consistent executive support. One thing that is certain is that at the heart of any effective company-wide program is employee acceptance. This is especially true with an initiative such as this, in which the knowledge and experience of every employee becomes paramount to identifying and dealing with risks at an early stage.

According to the Treasury Board of Canada, an organization demonstrates continuous learning with respect to risk management if the following conditions have been met[1]:

- An appropriate risk management culture is fostered.
- Learning is linked to risk management strategy at many levels.
- Responsible risk taking and learning from experience is encouraged and supported.
- There is considerable information sharing as the basis for decision making.
- Decision making includes a range of perspectives including the views of stakeholders, employees, and citizens.
- Input and feedback are actively sought and are the basis for further action.

Employees cooperate with a company as part of their social contract for a number of reasons: money, security, comradeship, interest, status, and even loyalty. However, invariably, to function at their maximum effectiveness, employees at any level in the organization have the need for two important things: clarity and credit.

Almost every employee at any level will accept the need for legal and ethical behavior. The challenge for management is to convey the absolute necessity of that ethical behavior in the face of day-to-day pressures on employees to perform and achieve targets. Obviously, asking employees to consciously balance ethical behavior (long-term good) against the pressures of time and the need to perform at high expectations (short-term good) becomes even more difficult in a culture in which any dissenting voices are seen as negative and counterproductive, that is, where employees are only expected to give "110 percent," without question. The difficulty, as Debra Amidon, founder and chief executive officer (CEO) of Entovation points out, is that "we remain steeped in the traditions of competitive strategy, as individuals, teams, enterprises, and entire nations. The creation of a truly collaborative culture is consequently an extremely challenging task."[2]

In this new era of business, company executives can no longer afford to preside over a business culture in which employees willingly and obediently commit unethical acts. In that culture, an ethical framework simply becomes nothing more than a legal protection exercise.

"Many companies now understand that corporate social responsibility cannot flourish in an environment where innovation and independent thinking are not welcome," observes Business for Social Responsibility. "In a similar vein, there must also be a commitment to close the gap between what the company says it stands for and the reality of its actual performance. Goals and aspirations should be ambitious, but care should be exercised so the company says what it means and means what it says. A 1999 Arthur Andersen report found that having an ethics and compliance program that employees perceive to exist only to protect the reputation of top management may be more harmful than having no program at all."[3]

These types of corporate cultures, endemic particularly in the United States where making the numbers at every level every quarter is seen as all important, undermine much of the effectiveness of an ethical knowledge and risk management (KRM) framework. Given that employees take their cue from leadership, if management accepts the business case for early risk identification and ethical behavior by its employees, it will have to convey that to employees in a positive and unambiguous way.

"If you're going to have the kind of pressure that'll make decent people go wrong," says Carl Skooglund from Texas Instruments, "you'll find it in the employee-supervisor relationship. There are two ways that the employee-supervisor relationship can really go wrong: one, if you set goals that realistically cannot be met, and two, if you have an environment where the employee is made to feel that failure is totally unacceptable."[4]

Thomas White, a specialist in corporate ethics, agrees. "When the cost of failure is too high, people feel enormous pressure to compromise both their own values and the company's stated standards. And for all practical purposes, it's an employee's supervisor who determines the cost of failure."[5]

As we have seen, there need not be a conflict between profit and good behavior, but employees simply need to understand what is expected of them. That is why communication of a clearly written set of value statements and code of conduct—endorsed and delivered by senior management—is so important. Combined with an unambiguous set of activities for analyzing and reporting on risk, most employees will welcome the clarity and the opportunity to contribute.

The second thing that is important to all employees is that they receive credit (e.g., compensation, praise, or status) for their efforts. This doesn't always have to be tied directly to compensation and performance appraisals (although that helps a lot) but can be manifested in simple approval and recognition from their managers and peers. Whatever the format, it is integral to changing attitudes and ensuring widespread acceptance.

For most companies that have been working on initiatives in this area, the key to successful employee acceptance comes primarily from four (arguably) straightforward techniques for ensuring success of these types of programs:

- Communication
- Education and training
- Incorporating risk and knowledge sharing into day-to-day operational activities
- Incentive programs

The Communications Program

The importance of a formal process of employee education and communication has been demonstrated many times during the past decade as companies have made dramatic structural changes or implemented International Organization for Standardization (ISO) standards or Enterprise Resource Planning (ERP) systems.

This high level of communication and training is valuable in several ways. First, and most obviously, it educates employees and effectively conveys corporate values and the importance of behaving ethically. The process also teaches employees important personal skills, such as team cooperation, analytical skills, and the need to take personal responsibility for the day-to-day activities that can affect the good name of the company. And because every employee is trained uniformly, there is the added advantage of a common language and purpose. Every employee should know how to access information on standards or compliance requirements and to discuss or report violations. Discussions on risk should become routine and businesslike and not be seen as exceptional or accusatorial.

This communication policy is important as well because it provides the clarity that all employees require about the often complex and conflicting pressures of balancing "making the numbers" with an ethical code of conduct. Employees cannot be expected to intuitively understand how to effectively balance productivity with probity and open-ness, and nothing causes greater resentment in an employee than being held accountable for policies or behavior that is inconsistent or unexpressed.

Because these company-wide programs are not without cost and disruption, the fact that senior leadership is willing to make that type of investment demonstrates to all employees that the corporation takes the issues or ethics and risk management seriously. Moreover, a good communication program demonstrates to the outside world that the company is fulfilling its legal responsibilities, something that is increasingly important under strict U.S. sentencing guidelines.

Two-Way Communications with Stakeholders

Something that we have learned over the past decade with enterprise-wide programs is that an effective corporate communications program is not simply telling employees what is expected of them. A good com-munications policy is ongoing and actively seeks (in fact is dependent upon) input from employees and various parties interested in the outcome of policy.

For that reason, the communication process should also extend to various stakeholders who in the past may not have been considered part of corporate policy making. These include all the parties who might be affected by corporate activities: suppliers, investors, analysts, and non-governmental organizations (NGOs) and local communities. In fact, the more these many different and often conflicting parties can be con-sulted in the development of the risk decision-making process the better. Two-way communication (i.e., asking their opinion and keeping them informed of policies) goes a long way to curbing knee-jerk reac-tions when volatile issues arise. It also helps to address one of the prob-lems that often plagues a risk management review: understanding the gap between perceptions and reality in any situation.

In fact, this stakeholder dialogue is one of the fundamental tenets of the AccountAbility 1000 (AA 1000) approach and is one of the reasons why an effective risk management process can be strengthened by the methodical approach that comes through the use of these types of standards.

Executive Education

Finally, there should be a communication policy for senior management and board members. Too often senior leadership actually does not understand what the company is doing to promote an ethical culture or to identify risks. At the outset, senior officers of the corporation should meet in an executive alignment workshop, specifically dedicated to the subject of an integral program of ethics and KRM. Most large companies will find this difficult to manage, but there are many important reasons why companies need to overcome their natural tendency to avoid investing precious time in these types of workshops among its senior leaders. In the first place, it helps all executives to get on the same page so they all understand exactly why the program is needed and what it involves. It also allows them a structured but informal environment to discuss their concerns, to clarify ambiguities, and to come to a consensus on the business case, resources, and approach. Most executives will probably believe that the company already has a strong ethical and risk management approach, and if the company doesn't and they need to understand that, there can be nothing more valuable than this type of alignment workshop.

The communications policy also needs to involve the board of directors, a group that is too often excluded from direct involvement in these types of efforts. After all, the purpose of the board of directors is oversight, and there should be no greater concern to them than making certain that the company is managing risks well. One of the most often-cited issues with regard to recent scandals was that board members had no sense of the complexities or activities occurring in the company that they were being paid to oversee.

Directors are used to flipping through Audit Committee reports and nodding sagely, not asking questions in fear of looking out of touch or ignorant. One thing that I have always found is that both at the senior executive and the board level, people are often afraid to ask questions, even though the ability to fulfill their management and oversight function is dependent upon a thorough understanding of the situation. Senior leadership needs to understand what the process for risk management is and to understand its role in that process.

"The most effective and profitable operation of the company," contends Martha Clark Goss, director at Foster Wheeler, "is usually a board's prime interest, which it should be. But there are times when it is not clear how a board member can have a direct impact on effective management of the company without engaging in micromanagement. The best way to solve this dilemma is to place more of a focus on ensuring that a well-structured strategic risk management plan exists and is operating effectively."[6]

Tools for Communication

The methods used to communicate to various parties in this process can vary widely but usually include several things.

First, a statement from the CEO stressing the importance of the program, delivered either in person or videotaped. Texas Instruments, once again provides a good example.

"Let there be no mistake," explained the late Jerry Junkins, former CEO of Texas Instruments, on the corporate video shown to all employees. "We will not let the pursuit of sales, billings, or profits distort our ethical principles. We always have, and we always will, place integrity before shipping, before billings, before profits, before anything. If it comes down to a choice between making a desired profit and doing it right, you don't have a choice. You'll do it right."[7]

Some companies include a review of the progress of the ethics/risk program as a regular feature of their quarterly management and employee meetings, and many companies use ethics newsletters with specific or hypothetical examples of ethical dilemmas to reinforce the company's uncompromising stance on ethics. Hot-line policies and contact numbers should be made known. The intranet and internal portal in several progressive companies now have a sidebar, with links reserved specifically for ethical and risk issues.

Most companies also have the chief ethics and risk officer (CERO) make a series of "road-show" speeches to employees and various outside stakeholders, explaining the ethics program. Ray Mattholie, head of risk and insurance solutions at British Telecom, explains that he promotes their risk solutions department "as a 'center of excellence' to spread risk evaluation procedures through the company and 'disseminate a risk culture.' The department assists business units within the organization by laying the ground for risk management, with the aim to encourage more people to realize they are their own risk managers, with the department acting in a support capacity."[8]

Finally, it is also important as an integral part of the process itself to publish the company's efforts and accomplishments as part of a social and ethical accounting, auditing, and reporting (SEAAR) process. Initiatives like the Global Reporting Initiative have specific areas dedicated to allowing companies to demonstrate their efforts in communicating to internal and external stakeholders the company's ethical expectations.

Ethics and risk management are important to the company, to employees (whose pensions are often at risk), to the investment community, to NGOs, and to government regulators. Therefore, the more effective a company is in explaining its good policies (and authenticating them through third-party audits), the better for all concerned. It is the first step to overcoming the "greenwash" credibility gap that comes from unstandardized and unauthenticated claims of good corporate behavior.

EDUCATION AND TRAINING

Apart from communicating to employees and other stakeholders the organization's ethics/risk framework and process, leading companies also usually dedicate an education and training program specifically to address ethical and KRM issues with employees. This education program has to be much more substantive than the often cursory discussions that accompany the new-employee orientation at many companies, where employees are told not to steal, not to make photocopies for personal use, or not to use abusive language. Most companies provide a copy of their code of conduct to new employees, usually accompanied by a short presentation on the first morning of new-employee orientation. Leading practices in this area favor following up that initial presentation with a "risk and ethics workshop" attended by a mix of new and current employees, where the risk/ethics program is explained more fully.

As important as stressing key values and ethical guidelines to new employees may be, it is only after an employee is well ensconced in his or her personal role in the company that he or she will be able to appreciate possible ethical dilemmas or understand their role in everyday risk management. For that reason, ethical and risk management education is much more effective if it is provided to seasoned employees as part of a broader initiative.

HP/Compaq, for example, according to Debra Dunn, senior vice president, Corporate Affairs, not only provides all of its employees with extensive training in ethics and business conduct, but it also has an ethics audit that includes all of the key elements of a stage three company's ethical framework:

- A formal code of conduct
- Training in ethical decision making
- Formal and confidential channels to voice concern
- An ethics committee
- Discipline for misconduct
- Integrity emphasized to new employees
- Integrity modeled by senior management

HP/Compaq also has anonymous reporting procedures, and when issues do arise, it consults with various representatives from legal, human resources, and operational specialists.[9]

One of the key issues of ethics and risk management in today's corporation is the policy of document retention. E-mails, scanned photos, newspaper clippings and documents, calendars, and investigation notes all need to be either retained or destroyed according to consistent and ethical legal considerations. As we discuss in Chapter 10, a document retention policy is paramount to the success of risk and ethical management programs, and yet its effectiveness is largely dependent on the employees themselves. Training must provide clear and consistent guidance in this area.

These workshops should include exercises that help teams of attendees to understand in more depth the company's value statement, and code of conduct, and teach employees to identify and react to operational-level risks. They should also include information on the risk management process, a strategic-level presentation of possible legislative and regulatory issues facing the company, including health, safety, and environmental standards to which the company is held. And of course, the program should also explain how to get assistance on ethical issues or risks, and how to report—both through regular channels or if necessary confidentially—possible risks or infractions.

Much of this type of work can be organized and delivered by human resources staff in cooperation with the Risk and Ethics Committee members, who in most companies are increasingly taking on the burden for training and ethics issues. It may also be worthwhile to consider specialist ethics and risk management consultants, particularly for more in-depth training that is most meaningful when it is tailored to reflect real-life issues facing employees in different departments. Texas Instruments, for example, found that a video produced by an outside group could be too high-level to be of real value to employees and has created additional material that deals with specific business areas.

"One request we kept getting from our employees," explains Carl Skooglund, "was 'please individualize the material, make it something usable so that when I go back to my job tomorrow morning, I don't have just a bunch of high-level principles but some tools, something to use in the day-to-day dilemmas that I encounter.'"

In a study of the ethics programs of several prominent companies—Texas Instruments, Martin Marietta, General Dynamics—in the early 1990s, Thomas White, professor and director of the Center for Business Ethics at Loyola Marymount University, described his findings on codes of conduct and executive attitudes.

"In the same vein," says White, "Martin Marietta [in the early 1990s] developed a set of cases from within the company. They asked people from different parts of the organization to describe ethical problems they've faced, and they use these cases in their workshops along with some generic cases developed by groups working in line with the Defense Industry Initiative. . . . [They] also do separate workshops for every major function in the company: contracts, marketing, accounting, finance, procurement, quality control and manufacturing operations."[10]

INCORPORATING RISK AND KNOWLEDGE SHARING INTO DAY-TO-DAY OPERATIONAL ACTIVITIES

The ultimate goal of all of these exercises—the value statement, code of conduct, the application of international standards, risk management, and ethics education and training—is to develop a company culture that appreciates the need for ethical behavior and knowledge sharing so that ethical behavior and good risk management become integral to the company culture.

"This is absolutely vital," says John Dombrick, senior manager, Business Continuity and Emergency Planning, at British Airways. "It is only with such knowledge sharing that the impacts of risks that originate in one area can be known about in other areas that are impacted, before it is too late."[11]

If creating a knowledge-sharing culture is one of the ultimate goals of the program, there are other techniques—those that have been developed as part of knowledge management programs during the past few years—that can help. These include many of the techniques that we have already looked at, including the following:

- Making risk scanning an integral part of day-to-day operational meetings
- An accountability matrix
- Hard tagging for expert advice
- Knowledge mapping
- Incorporating "lessons learned" into a continuous learning program

REWARDS AND INCENTIVE PROGRAMS

Which brings us to the real area of difficulty in these programs, and that is developing an effective program for encouraging (i.e., rewarding) good risk and ethical behavior. Because employees at all levels require clarity and credit in their day-to-day activities, to be effective in driving the responsibility for ethics and risk management into the organizational culture, companies need to provide explicit direction to employees about what behavior is rewarded and what behavior will be penalized. As with all quality and improvement programs, the way in which a company recruits, compensates, and publicly recognizes employees will be one, if not the most, important way of ensuring that employees at all levels take ethical behavior seriously.

The problem with rewarding ethical behavior, of course, is that it is not something that should be seen as exceptional, and therefore it can be difficult to incorporate in a personal appraisal. And it is no easier to reward employees for confidential whistle-blowing (an obvious conflict of interest) or for not stealing, lying, or cheating.

"Everyone says it's a nice idea to reward people for ethical conduct," explained Kent Druyvesteyn, who was the director of General Dynamics' corporate ethics program, "but reward them for what? Telling the truth? Presumably that's expected. Telling on someone who doesn't tell the truth? That suggests a 'fink of the month' or 'rat of the year' award or even bounties. In ethics programs, we have a hard time thinking about how we show our support and gratitude for right conduct."[12]

This doesn't mean that a company can't incorporate required ethical behavior into job descriptions or even personal performance plans. After all, other soft areas such as "shares knowledge" or "works well in a team" are now an accepted part of most employees key performance indicators. What it does mean, however, is that an ever increasing portion of those performance indicators will be more or less "pass-fail" in nature, with "pass" meaning very little and "failure" possibly resulting in severe penalties. This also has the disadvantage of further diluting much of the "stretch" element of performance appraisal, by adding another set of performance measurements on which good behavior and active participation are rewarded as standard.

Providing incentives for good risk management behavior is slightly easier and more effective. After all, being an acceptably ethical employee is more passive than actively participating—attending training courses, being part of a hard-tagged knowledge network, highlighting risks or ethical gaps, contributing to an early alert team—in a risk management process. Risk management techniques all require time and effort and can easily be documented. This type of incentive is important, to encourage participation in the program itself.

In fact, incentives for supporting the ethical and risk management process become easier to implement at a managerial or supervisory level, in that organizational leaders can be expected to actively support and oversee education and training of their direct reports and to monitor and provide quantitative measurements for these types of activities as part of their role as manager.

"So far," explained Thomas White, "the only way this problem has been approached is that some companies are making a concern with ethics a regular part of a manager's responsibilities. General Dynamics has adopted the policy that managers and supervisors have special leadership responsibilities for implementing the ethics standards and will be measured in how well they carry out those responsibilities."[13]

Increasingly, it is becoming obvious that one of the most effective ways of encouraging ethical behavior, or behavior that falls within a company's level of risk tolerance, is simply to make certain that employees don't have unrealistic targets set for their normal operational duties. After all, even the best developed program for ethical conduct will be undermined if the overall organizational culture still invokes bad behavior by requiring too much of employees.

"Another major challenge in incorporating ethical values into an organization," contends White, "is to set objectives which stretch employees to the full extent of their capacities but do not push them to the point where they'll be tempted to meet them by wrong doing."[14]

What this discussion of rewards and objectives ultimately points to is the critical role that supervisors play in determining the ethical character of a company. It is interesting to note that in a survey of more than 300 managers completed by the National Institute of Business Management, the behavior of an employee's superiors was ranked as the second most important factor in influencing decision making. This was surpassed only by a personal code and outstripped the behavior of one's peers, formal company policy, and the ethical climate in the industry.

ENFORCEMENT

On the other hand, if the carrot is difficult, a company needs also to be careful about the stick. Enforcement policies are a necessary element of any ethical or risk management policy, and violations of the ethical code or legal or operational standards has to be met with some type of certain and fair penalty. On the other hand, a company must beware of the potential for abuse of the system by vengeful employees hoping to discredit company adversaries. Even worse, a company has to be careful to ensure that whistle-blowers and those who participate actively in the risk management program do not themselves become the victims of retaliation.

"Investigations and sanctions are a very important part of a program," points out Kent Druyvesteyn from General Dynamics, "because if you don't have them, a lot of people will think the program is nonsense."[15]

Simple compliance can usually be confirmed by making managers at all levels responsible for ensuring that their employees understand and are abiding by all ethical standards and rules. It is simple enough to make that part of a manager's incentive system through key performance indicators. Compliance (to OSHA or EPA standards or measured against SA 8000 or ISO 14001 type of standards) is much easier and can help pinpoint risk areas where repeated infringements indicate a significant managerial and operational failure.

Penalties for unethical or illegal behavior range from simple verbal or written warnings to suspensions, firing, or even criminal prosecution. Choosing which of these applies is, of course, the difficult part. To protect and support managers, it is important that serious infringements be reviewed and managed by the CERO, who can refer the issue to the Ethics Committee. This is the most equitable and effective way of managing sensitive and difficult issues.

A CULTURAL IMPERATIVE

In the end, the difficulty of providing effective incentive and reward programs simply highlights the need to integrate the several key elements of an enterprise-wide program that we have been discussing:

- An ethical framework including a value statement, code of conduct, and dedicated chief risk officer and crew
- Adherence to recognized reporting and behavior standards
- An integrated program of KRM
- Incentive programs

Creating a culture that values and guards integrity has to rely for success on a combination of all of these activities, but there is one more area that is part of the modern organization and inherent to KRM: systems for collecting, distributing, and comparing key information that is necessary for managing an ethical and risk process.

CHAPTER ENDNOTES

1 "Best Practices in Risk Management: Public and Private Sectors Internationally," Treasury Board of Canada Web site. Available from www.www.tbs-sct.gc.ca/pubs_pol/dcgpubs/riskmanagement/rm-pps2_e.html#_toc456660351.

2 Simon Lelic, " Managing Knowledge to Manage Risk," *Knowledge Management*, 6, no. 1 (September 2, 2002). Available from www.kmmagazine.com.

3 "Introduction to Corporate Social Responsibility," *Business for Social Responsibility* White Papers. Available from www.bsr.org.

4 Thomas White, "Ethics Incorporated: How America's Corporations Are Institutionalizing Moral Values," Center for Ethics and Business, Loyola Marymount University. Available from www.ethicsandbusiness.org/corpeth.htm.

5 Thomas White, "Ethics Incorporated: How America's Corporations Are Institutionalizing Moral Values," Center for Ethics and Business, Loyola Marymount University. Available from www.ethicsandbusiness.org/corpeth.htm.

6 Martha Clark Goss, "Are your executives doing enough to manage risk?" *Directorship*, October 1, 2002.

7 Thomas White, "Ethics Incorporated: How America's Corporations Are Institutionalizing Moral Values," Center for Ethics and Business, Loyola Marymount University. Available from www.ethicsandbusiness.org/corpeth.htm.

8 Ben Huut, "Profile: Ray Mattholie," *International Risk Management* 5, no. 9, (October 1998).

9 Debra Dunn, "Impact of the HP/Compaq Merger on Global Corporate Citizenship" (conference talk at How to Manage Corporate Responsibility seminar, October 4, 2002).

10 Thomas White, "Ethics Incorporated: How America's Corporations Are Institutionalizing Moral Values," Center for Ethics and Business, Loyola Marymount University. Available from www.ethicsandbusiness.org/corpeth.htm.

11 Simon Lelic, "Managing Knowledge to Manage Risk," *Knowledge Management*, 6, no. 1 (September 2, 2002). Available from www.kmmagazine.com.

[12] Tim Dickson, "The Financial Case for Behaving Responsibly," *Financial Times,* August 19, 2002, p. 5.

[13] Thomas White, "Ethics Incorporated: How America's Corporations Are Institutionalizing Moral Values," Center for Ethics and Business, Loyola Marymount University. Available from www.ethicsandbusiness.org/corpeth.htm.

[14] Thomas White, "Ethics Incorporated: How America's Corporations Are Institutionalizing Moral Values," Center for Ethics and Business, Loyola Marymount University. Available from www.ethicsandbusiness.org/corpeth.htm.

[15] Thomas White, "Ethics Incorporated: How America's Corporations Are Institutionalizing Moral Values," Center for Ethics and Business, Loyola Marymount University. Available from www.ethicsandbusiness.org/corpeth.htm.

TEN

Systems That Support Integrated Knowledge and Risk Management

Information technology (IT) is now at the heart of the modern corporation, and those companies that have established truly effective knowledge and risk management (KRM) frameworks have usually employed several IT systems to help them capture, distribute, analyze, and record relevant information as part of a broader knowledge management program. Those systems usually are a combination of several common platforms found in most modern companies:

- The organization's intranet for communication
- Access for employees to the Internet and the Web for external information
- Knowledge management systems for identifying company experts and decision makers and providing them with necessary information and contacts
- A central database structure for storing and retrieving documents and data
- Decision-support systems
- Multiple specialist systems and databases for risk and incident management
- Environmental health and safety (EHS)–compliance systems

- Customer service and customer resource management (CRM) systems

Each of these systems is important in an integrated KRM approach, and most are already available in one form or another in stage two companies. A company can truly begin to manage its risk in the most effective way only when these systems are used as part of a KRM approach.

Systems for Knowledge and Risk Management

Most stage two companies have already implemented many of the systems that make up a strong KRM foundation. Any U.S.-based company that manufactures or assembles products, for example, will have some system in place that helps to monitor compliance with Occupational Safety and Health Administration (OSHA) or Environmental Protection Agency (EPA) requirements. A corporate call center, particularly when supported by a CRM system, can provide customer service agents with a valuable tool for capturing customer concerns on product safety issues, and these customer service agents will often be the first to learn of growing public disquiet over a particular aspect of corporate policy. CRM systems can also help to capture and distribute that type of information immediately to the chief ethics and risk officer (CERO) and can provide early alert teams with valuable electronic data concerning reported incidents.

Many companies have also implemented environmental safety systems, which are increasingly becoming the foundation for broader risk management programs. Of course, all stage two companies have Internet access, and usually an intranet, with internal communications, groupware, search, and e-mail facilities. These are, after all, arguably the most fundamental and effective technologies for sharing knowledge and gathering information. Many companies have more specialized knowledge management systems, such as knowledge mapping modules, a lessons-learned database, or decision-support tools.

However, as we have seen, most stage two companies have still not integrated these systems in a way that allows for a strong program of KRM. Seldom, for example, have companies initiated a formal review process for spotting potential crises areas or for early alert of potential problems. Most do not record incidents or track them to see corporate-wide trends. Even fewer take the next step and attempt to predict and develop preemptive policy.

"Reputation risk management requires a knowledge solution that is enterprise-wide in scope and scale," says Jim Kartalia. "To fit this need, the technology solutions used must embrace the entire enterprise and be leading edge, knowledge-based, and easy to learn and use."[1]

IT Systems Available in the Modern Organization

The Internet, the Web, and a Company's Intranet

The most valuable knowledge management IT tool may well be the software that is now universal in all companies: e-mail, groupware, and access to the Web via the Internet. These systems can provide most of the important functions required for ongoing knowledge management tasks, providing a secure network for communication and data collection and storage. The standard features of these systems (i.e., groupware, e-mail, search engines, shared applications, and document-storage and common retrieval functionality) help employees to work collaboratively in virtual teams, regardless of their geography.

Access to the Internet through browsers and search engines can provide employees with information on political, legislative, and commercial issues or best-practice techniques. And, of course, the company intranet is an effective way of communicating standard operating procedures, risk management objectives, and ethical policy to both employees and suppliers or for contacting and briefing members of the hard-tagged knowledge network when an incident arises. This versatile framework also provides the integral system logic for mapping, indexing, relating, and finding information through browsers and search engines, which is so crucial to the knowledge management process.

Knowledge Management Systems

Knowledge management software applications can provide a company with special functionality that can be used as part of a KRM platform; these include the following:

Specialized search tools: These allow employees throughout the company to quickly find documented information not only on the Internet but particularly in company databases and repositories.

External business research and analysis and reputation management tools: These include specialist databases for subjects or industries, access to professional research and industry reports, and contacts with global specialists outside the company.

Knowledge-mapping tools: These provide skills databases, knowledge-mapping functions, and tools that can identify company employees with similar or recent incident experience, or certification and training in specialist areas. These tools can complete a knowledge gap analysis for defining education and training needs and can provide a useful escalation process so that a priority query is instantly distributed to a group of experts and company executives to ensure a rapid response.

Collaboration tools: Online collaboration becomes important during an early alert team or incident investigation or when drawing in opinions from "hard-tagged" specialists scattered around the company. These systems include mechanisms for simultaneous screen viewing and live online conversations.

Capturing leading practice and lessons learned: Template-based tools make it easy for employees to input key lessons learned in a standardized format to a central repository.

Administrative tools for measuring system usage and tracking trends: These allow knowledge management specialists to monitor and "tune" systems depending on need, effectiveness, and usage statistics.

Records Retention

Over the past decade, as IT advances have made it possible to gain access to ever increasing amounts of information, the greatest problems have come from information overload and our inability to manage and interpret that information in a way that it is meaningful to the recipient, whether that is a line worker or the chief operating officer.

Document organization and retention policies are therefore at the heart of an effective KRM process. There are countless stories of executives explaining that the key information that could have helped to alert them to potential risks (e.g., missed maintenance activities, illegal storage of toxic substances, health inspection warnings, or emissions violations) is that the information was simply lost or at least never captured in the information jungle. The sheer volume of information that is created every day within the modern company means that an organization needs an effective way of deciding what information to destroy, what to retain, and how to organize that which remains for easy retrieval.

This is particularly true when investigating a particular risk area or when an incident has developed into legal action that may require extra care in information collection. Any event that is likely to lead to an investigation or require a detailed explanation of what the company knew, when, and what it did in response will require an effective system of document retention and retrieval. Consider the e-mails, faxed documents, scanned newspaper articles, inspection reports, conference videos, meeting minutes, photos, spreadsheets, and Web pages that will be relevant to ongoing incident management investigation if it becomes part of a legal discovery process.

This can all be expensive and time consuming, but it is unavoidable and in the event of a legal investigation can mean the difference between a strong defense and accusations of hiding and destroying evidence. Legal difficulties can arise suddenly once a suit is filed and the company is placed into the discovery process, where the corporation must produce all "relevant" information to the charges. In fact, one of the most prominent strategies pursued by lawyers these days is simply to request documents during the discovery process, with the almost certain knowledge the corporations will be unable to produce them. This approach can work with devastating effect on a jury, where a company's incompetence or indifference in document retention can quickly be turned into accusations of not only violating legal requirements (shows sloppy and negligent management) or worse, purposely destroying documents that might indicate the company's guilt.

The former accountancy giant Andersen is a good example of how badly things can go wrong if the company does not have a formal and ethical document-retention and -destruction plan in place (or does not adhere to it). Federal officials alleged that from October 23 through November 8, 2001, when the Securities and Exchange Commission (SEC) served Andersen with an Enron-related subpoena, the company pursued a "wholesale destruction of documents," shredding documentation and deleting computer files related to its activities with Enron. Although only fined $500,000, the audit firm's reputation was undermined to such an extent that the company was essentially ruined in a matter of days.

A recent litigant against British American Tobacco (BAT) was awarded by a jury $350,000 when a judge found that BAT had systematically destroyed documents concerning what the company knew about the addictive nature of nicotine and of the impact of smoking on health generally. "The predominant purpose of the document destruction," the judge found, "was the denial to plaintiffs of information which was likely to be of importance in proving their case." Although BAT argues that it was free to shred documents that might be helpful to litigants in the future, the judge ruled ominously that "while corporations are not obligated to store documents indefinitely, they are not free to destroy them in anticipation of future litigation."

And, of course, in 2002, five Wall Street firms, including Goldman Sachs and CitiGroup, were fined a combined total of more than $8.3 million for failing to save e-mails as required by state and federal regulatory authorities.[2]

This conservative attitude toward document retention seems to be changing, observes Jim Kartalia, chief executive officer (CEO) of Entegra. "Two or three years ago, we would go to an enterprise and end up talking to their legal department and it was right away, 'oh my God, we can't document that type of thing, it will all come out in the deposition.' Our point was, listen, whether it is centralized or decentralized, that information is still in your company—in a Word document, in an e-mail, or a spreadsheet—the investigators are going to find it and you're going to look like you're guilty of withholding information. And under the sentencing guidelines, penalties are much greater if a corporation is not openly providing that information."

"For that reason," he concludes, "recently we have seen less of that sort of response and a move toward real transparency. At least if your information is centralized, a company can provide all the relevant e-mails and documents without having to tear apart the company's whole information system in order to find them."[3]

On the other hand, much of the miscellaneous detritus of everyday business doesn't need to be kept and only means added cost and a greater likelihood of information overload. To be both cost-effective and legally, practically, and ethically compliant, it will take more than a policy of just saving everything. And yet most company employees still have no idea what the company's records-retention policy is and therefore seldom adhere to it.

It is a complex subject, and there are many good books and consultants who can help a company with document-retention and content management policies. Nonetheless, when developing a KRM process for the company, one should acknowledge several guiding principles about a document-retention policy:

- The program needs to be clearly defined, consistent, and auditable.
- It should take into consideration legal and regulatory requirements, for example, which documents are required to be retained under law and for how long.
- It is worthwhile considering what documents need to be gathered generically for decision making when reacting to an identified risk.
- It is important to know what types of information need to be destroyed for confidentiality reasons.

A document- and information-retention policy also needs to be ongoing; it will need to be reviewed and changed periodically as regulations and policies change. It also needs to provide consistency throughout the corporation and among all different departments while taking into account differences in information and regulatory requirements for different functions, states, or countries.

One of the most often cited problems in this area is that responsibility for record management is diffuse, with no single person or group (IT, corporate librarian, human resources, or legal) responsible for policy review and audit. For that reason, many companies are moving to incorporate document-retention responsibility into the function of the CERO.

Whatever the policy, it is going to be primarily dependent for its success on the employees themselves. This will mean integrating content management and document-retention policies into your enterprise-wide risk and ethics program, with appropriate communication and training. Much of the success of any document-retention program, after all, is going to be dependent on individual employee discretion. Therefore, clear guidance on policy also needs to be supported with a logical explanation of the process so that employees understand why they need to make a considered effort to adhere to the policy. Employees are much more likely to comply if they understand the logic of what to keep and what to discard.

Obviously, none of this can simply be left to trust. As part of risk management, a company needs to provide a method for auditing and ensuring compliance with these policies. This usually goes well beyond current stage one and stage two company practice, where employees are simply asked to acknowledge that they understand the guidelines as part of reading and acknowledging the code of conduct.

Ultimately, although the cost and effort for retention will be considerable, it is practically, ethically, and legally unavoidable, and as costly as it may seem, it will be significantly less expensive than the risk associated with being accused of losing, or worse, purposely destroying relevant documents and e-mails. Even market analysts now view the way a company maintains its records as a reflection of its management competence, and in these days of scandal, potential trustworthiness.

Environmental Management Information Systems and Integrated Risk Management Software

Environmental management information systems (EMISs) are, in terms of ethics and risk management, one of the more important suites of software tools that have emerged in the past 5 years. These systems usually provide a variety of important environmental tracking and performance tools, including legislative change notifications and flexible report generators for tracking a company's performance or nonconformance against state and federal environmental (and sometimes health and safety) requirements. Most systems also provide tools that help a company to track energy usage, recycling efforts, and emissions, so it can monitor costs and create efficiencies where possible.

Recently, these EMISs have begun to expand to take on much of the functionality of a fuller risk management system, providing additional features that go beyond just resource or energy compliance and efficiency monitoring. In keeping with the emerging requirements for social and ethical accounting, auditing, and reporting

(SEAAR)–type reporting, several progressive companies now provide modules for measuring, managing, and reporting on other issues such as employment rights performance and even corporate governance standards.

The Entropy System, an enterprise-wide risk management system based on an EHS foundation produced by Entropy International, is a good example. "The Entropy System," says Hewitt Roberts, the company's CEO, "is moving into total risk management. Although its original foothold was in environmental safety monitoring, there is a natural built-in transition into any of the other risk disciplines, whether that is ethical sourcing and [Social Accountability] SA 8000 or security and 7799 and on down the chain through the full umbrella of what would be covered under corporate governance and risk management."

"The Entropy System is based off of the framework for [International Organization for Standardization] ISO 14000, so the initial assessment provides the company with a benchmark in relation to environmental, health, and safety, employees, shareholders, and ethical sourcing. It then provides all planning and action tools to improve performance and a framework for managing all the documents required to improve policies, procedures, set objectives and build action plans, and then finally to audit and correct performance if it is noncompliant. If there is an issue, the system automatically raises a 'nonconformance' flag. . . . Inherent in ISO are the same audit, management reviews and action plans."[4]

These robust, integrated, enterprise-wide risk management systems can provide not only access to a central repository of all risk management–related documents, but also to tools for mapping, ranking, and tracking risks, identifying stakeholders and specialists, and monitoring the steps being taken to contain the risk. These systems can even be proactive and dynamic, helping to provide early warning of developing issues and alerting those responsible for managing risks in a particular area. At a minimum, these systems have five major functions, which are discussed in the following sections.

Communications Functions

One of the key features of any enterprise system is its ability to communicate broadly with employees and stakeholders. Most systems provide a portal on the company's intranet site that maintains various links to company news, issue alerts, legislative changes, or company policies and programs. These tools make it easy for employees to locate standard operating procedures and leading practice guidelines and can be used to post press reports or company position statements on issues or incidents.

Most suites also provide a "chat page" forum, specifically allocated to issues of ethics and risk, which can be invaluable as part of a way to identify potential issues from employees anywhere in the company, worldwide.

Risk Management Functions

Enterprise risk management software platforms usually also provide a variety of day-to-day risk management tools. These include the following:

- Audit and nonconformance alerts, which means that issues are immediately flagged for action and can be monitored through resolution by those in various departments or management ranks
- Customizable risk-"mapping" tools for deciding what issues need to be monitored, allowing process owners to identify and map risks in their responsibility areas
- Tools that help management to set and monitor individual and unit key performance indicators
- Various features for day-to-day management of compliance reporting, including a complete submission history of documentation, preformatted OSHA and EHS forms, and prompts for follow-up documentation

- A searchable relational database and repository for all risk-related information

Incident Management Tools

Once an incident has happened, organizations need to have tools in place specifically for tracking, managing, and resolving the situation. These incident management systems provide all the relevant information to various parties involved with a particular incident automatically and consistently and act as a repository for the complete record of events from investigation to close. They help to collect relevant information, including the following:

- A description of the circumstances
- Employees involved
- Assets, projects, or departments involved or affected
- Resources needed for resolution
- Possible repercussions
- Likely costs
- Actions taken
- Resolution activities and closing audits

They also guide a company through the steps necessary to manage resolution, including access to a responsibility matrix that identifies and contacts key decision makers in the incident resolution process, and a "contact manager" feature for identifying and contacting hard-tagged experts, both within the company and among outside experts.

Decision-Support Tools

One of the greatest challenges for the modern company is being able to take advantage of all the information-collection possibilities that exist with new technologies—information on internal operations, on current emissions policies, on safety violations, or concerns raised by employees—and to manage and interpret all of this information in a way that is of value to many different groups within the company.

Decision-support tools help to filter and prioritize information from various sources—EHS or CRM systems, e-mails, incident management systems, or strategic (procurement) sourcing software—and to manipulate the data in different ways in order to perform risk analysis, risk prioritization, and "what if" scenario planning. These systems can be set to focus on key environmental, financial, or social performance indicators and can provide benchmark comparisons between different factories, facilities, and suppliers.

Business Metabolics, for example, provides a software suite that provides an "insight engine," designed to capture and interpret "hard-to-understand" data for decision makers. Selected by Nike as a tool for helping it better understand how its overseas factory partners compare in terms of environmental and employment rights performance, the Business Metabolics suite provides executives with a process for taking operating data and transforming it into graphs, charts, and executive reports, essentially turning the reporting process into a decision-making tool.

Reporting Tools

One of the most important features of these systems is their ability to produce customizable reports for the various parties involved in the risk management process, such as risk managers, operational process owners, management, or board members. These tools can be configured to use relevant information and combine various display formats, graphs, and diagrams.

Entegra, for example, has an enterprise risk management system known as Ki4, which provides most of the aforementioned risk management features, including more than 220 preconfigured reports and

70 query functions so that managers can view risk data in ways that are most meaningful to them. The system also provides an interface to other applications, including all the standard spreadsheets and data-processing packages.

"Ki4 Risk and Reputation System is an enterprise technology solution," explains Jim Kartalia, Entegra's CEO, "that provides executives and managers with an 'early warning system' to organize all data associated with corporate incidents and issues."

"These risk reports that are produced by Ki4 go to the ethics committees of companies and can literally be reviewed in 10 minutes a day, keeping the company informed about any issues that have come up over the last 24 hours."[5]

Similarly, Entropy International has created a Web- and intranet-based enterprise system known as The Entropy System, which has evolved from EHS management to broader areas of general risk management. Demonstrating the inherent relationship between risk management and quality management, the system helps clients to become certified under a variety of internationally recognized standards, including ISO 14001, Eco-Management and Audit Scheme (EMAS), ISO 9000:2000, Occupational Health and Safety Administration Standard (OHSAS) 18001, and many of the emerging corporate social responsibility standards.

"The Entropy System," says Hewitt Roberts, the company CEO, "enables an organization to manage according to any of these Deming-cycle approaches to risk management, and because it is real time and IT-based, it is easy to report and verify performance."[6]

CHAPTER ENDNOTES

[1] Entegragroup.com Web site.

[2] Russell Mokhiber and Robert Weissman, "Bad Apples in a Rotten System," *Multinational Monitor*, 23, no. 12 (December 2002). Available from multinationalmonitor.org/mm2002/02december/dec02corp1.html.

³ Jim Kartalia, interviewed by the author, January 23, 2003.

⁴ Hewitt Roberts, interviewed by the author, February 13, 2003.

⁵ Jim Kartalia, interviewed by the author, January 23, 2003.

⁶ Hewitt Roberts, interviewed by the author, February 13, 2003.

ELEVEN
Choosing and Implementing Standards

Developing an ethical framework forms the central foundation of the company's risk management program. A strong program of knowledge and risk management (KRM) helps to identify, manage, and if done well, prevent unethical or illegal behavior in an organization. However, as with the accounting practices, a standardized set of rules concerning specific behavior and company performance and how to account for and report on that behavior and performance is necessary in order to provide the company, its investors, and regulators with reliable information from which to judge a company's future success. In short, an ethical framework is essential to set forth a company's principles but alone will not provide the necessary level of detail for behavior guidelines at an operational level. The next step is to make that ethical behavior objective, verifiable, and reportable. This is best done through a combined application of standards-based performance measurement and reporting.

Financial accounting standards and reporting, of course, have been enshrined in the business world for many years. They help bring confidence and stability to investors, providing crucial information needed to make decisions on investments. Often criticized for providing only a limited historical (and possibly massaged) view of a company's performance, it is usually left to investment analysts to consider other key factors—that is, the intangible measures that matter—that actually reflect the future potential of a company but are not easily compared or reported on objectively and are certainly not revealed through a company's financial statements. These include softer issues such as management vision, employee morale, a culture of integrity, and management processes to guard against undue risk.

When analyzing business performance through financial reports alone, however, three important areas of company behavior that should be captured and analyzed still remain largely unreported: corporate governance, environmental reporting, and social reporting. These are the focus of a recent and powerful movement for including these elements in company reports.

WHAT IS SOCIAL AND ETHICAL ACCOUNTING, AUDITING, AND REPORTING?

During the past 10 years, much has been made of social and intellectual capital; the logical next step is to measure a company's "integrity capital," where a corporation is able to objectively report on nonfinancial performance concerning areas such as their corporate governance, human rights, and environmental policies. As we have seen, now and increasingly in the future, how a company behaves in these areas will have a direct bearing not only on how it is perceived by analysts and shareholders, but also on how it is treated by customers, regulators, and pressure groups. In KPMG's terms, "Organizations are increasingly being asked to share their values as well as their value." This means that companies need to begin to integrate their nonfinancial and financial performance together in their annual reports.[1]

In the past, the criteria for what was "good" performance with regard to corporate governance or social or environmental behavior (particularly in developing markets that had few enforceable laws governing these types of things) was largely undefined. However, as multinational corporations expanded their supply chain, relocating their manufacturing base to lower wage, developing world markets over the past two decades, many companies came under fire from nongovernmental organizations (NGOs) and pressure groups for what appeared to be (and often obviously was) exploitation of the natural and human resources of poorer countries. Companies attempted to defend themselves against these charges, initially by producing media statements but more often by producing social and environmental reports that they devised on their own. These reports, in turn, came under criticism from pressure groups, who claimed that the criteria- and information-gathering processes that had been used by companies in compiling these reports were subjective and unaudited. In short, far too unreliable to provide any real assessment of the company's behavior in these areas to satisfy investors or pressure group campaigners.

As with other improvement movements in the past several decades, collaborative efforts began to grow among companies, industry coalitions, NGOs, unions, and other interested parties, hoping to establish broader more consistent and verifiable standards for social, environmental, and corporate governance reporting. These groups, and there are many, have attempted to develop guidelines for nonfinancial, ethical accounting principles, and measurements that corporations can adopt and for which certifiable compliance will provide a company with an objective "stamp of approval" that will be available to consumers and shareholders. As with quality movements, such as International Organization for Standardization 9000 [ISO 9000] and Six Sigma, there has been a good deal of early chaos as groups have attempted to come to agreement on both the procedures and the measurements that constitute an international standard.

In fact, for anyone just becoming familiar with social and environmental auditing standards and reporting, it may still appear uncoordinated and chaotic. In many ways that is true. Like any global standards development process, there are competing groups with different interests and priorities, coming from different industries and cultures. Accordingly there tends to be a good deal of confusion when it comes to the many new reporting and performance standards that are emerging. However, despite early disagreement, an auditable set of standards has begun to emerge.

This nonfinancial performance assessment and reporting can appear under many names, depending on its focus. Sometimes it is known as *sustainability reporting*, which emphasizes social, environmental, and economic performance, with the economic portion reflecting the overall impact or "footprint" that a company makes on the world. *Sustainability* as a phrase has become something of a catch-all and is used to describe policies that can include areas as diverse as biodiversity, water use, emissions, and climate change, and even broader topics such as income inequality and open trade policies.

Arguably the most useful description or label is still *SEAAR*, which stands for *social and ethical accounting, auditing, and reporting*, although the business press today also use the term triple–bottom-line accounting, reflecting an organization's combined reporting on financial, social, and environmental performance and emphasizing the important relationship between these three areas. They all more or less reflect the same thing, a growing set of tools and standards that can be used by companies to monitor and report on various types of nonfinancial performance.

Nonfinancial reporting itself is not a new concept, but it has only taken on a real authority in the last 5 years, bolstered by the globalization and exploitation issues that we looked at in earlier chapters. In fact, according to the Global Reporting Initiative (GRI), there are now more than 2500 companies that provide some type of environmental or sustainability report each year, including about half of the companies in the Global Fortune 250. This flurry of reporting activity has come, most people recognize, as a direct result of external pressure from activists, NGOs, investors, the press, and public for companies to improve their corporate behavior and to demonstrate a greater level of corporate "responsibility."

In the past 2 years particularly, there has been an enormous increase in the number of companies adopting standards and providing nonfinancial reports. And as might be expected, these still vary widely between company and industry. A recent KPMG survey found that all of the chemicals and synthetic companies listed in the Global

Financial Times 250 provided some type of SEAAR reporting in 2002; as did 86 percent of petrochemical companies, 84 percent of electronics and computer firms, 73 percent of automotive, and 58 percent of all oil and gas companies. The number of top Financial Times 100 companies issuing reports increased from 24 percent in 1999 to 30 percent in 2002.[2]

Why are standards important? Unfortunately, despite the positive trend, an independent company sustainability report is often not the same thing as either triple–bottom-line accounting or SEAAR in any formal sense, because these types of reports still tend to be long on "warm and fuzzy" text, with pictures of happy employees and glistening rain forests, and very short on any objective or auditable performance figures. In addition, as might be expected, they still tend to be focused much more on philanthropic efforts and community recycling initiatives, possibly worthy activities in themselves but not actually very valuable when trying to understand a company's genuine social or environmental performance or at deciphering potential risks in these areas that the company faces in the future.

Part of the reason that companies have been compelled to produce these sustainability reports is simply that for all the reasons we examined in earlier chapters, they feel pressure from NGOs, pressure groups, and their competition to prove that they are good corporate citizens. They have therefore rushed out their own publications, with little real rigor or standardization, tending to "cherry pick" what they discuss, promoting admirable activities, and leaving out questionable behavior altogether. In that sense, far too many of these reports are or at least are perceived to be still largely self-promotional "greenwash."

These reports, of course, should not be completed merely to placate pressure groups. They should be seen as an important part of the overall process by which a modern company explains its performance to the outside world, particularly to the investment community. In fact, putting aside for a moment the very real concerns of many NGO activists for protection of human and environmental rights and concentrating on the investment community, shareholders want to know four things from a company:

- (Genuine) financial performance
- Future plans that might affect profits, including new products, ventures, or board and leadership changes
- How well the corporation is managing risky ventures and avoiding unethical activities that might cause market instability, loss of reputation, or significant penalties
- How well decision makers understand what is taking place in the organization

Obviously, of these four broad areas, only the first two involve traditional financial and business reporting. Areas three and four involve more intangible information and fall more broadly into the areas of risk and knowledge management, ethical, social, and environmental reporting.

It takes only a quick review of recent scandals (e.g., Enron, Tyco, Merrill Lynch, Global Crossing, or WorldCom) to appreciate that quarterly financial reports can often mislead us into believing that a company is prospering when it isn't. Profitability (particularly when there is every incentive to create methods to ensure that these appear to remain high) can often be artificially altered to hide significant issues. And although nonfinancial reporting can be just as capricious, there is a growing recognition that a broader set of performance indicators are needed in order to assess the health of a company than those provided simply by a financial statement.

It is not only the activist and investor communities that are driving the move toward better standards and broader reporting, though. Many companies, or at least those that are now in stages three or four, are beginning to appreciate the operational value from these types of nonfinancial initiatives. Not only can they use these efforts to generate goodwill among those communities, but more often companies are finding that measuring and monitoring their performance against standards in areas such as employee satisfaction and energy efficiency, also helps them to improve their own productivity (Figure 11.1). As Jim Collins points out in his books *Good to Great* and *Built to Last*, the most successful companies are those that have a strong sense of purpose, that is, those that stand for something more than just making money. By focusing on that broader purpose, in the long run they bring a far greater return to their shareholders and employees.

There are many advantages that can come from this type of social and environmental reporting, including:

- Making the company focus on important social and environmental issues
- Helping the company to monitor trends in social and environmental performance that can reveal careless or risky processes

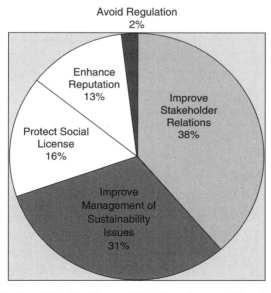

Benefits From SEAAR

FIGURE 11.1   *Benefits from SEAAR. (Source: "GlobeScan Survey of Sustainability Experts," Environics International, August 2002)*

- Verifying company claims for being socially responsible
- Promoting goodwill among stakeholders and employees

And of course, I would contend, these guidelines provide an equally important advantage to a company. They help to establish the framework for an integrity and risk strategy, processes, and culture, by:

- Helping the company to monitor trends and risk indicators in key operational, environmental, and social performance areas
- Providing a structure for aligning behavior and processes with their stated values and code of conduct
- Reporting more accurately to shareholders on the company's progressive activities

Of course, to be of any value to the investor community or to satisfy demanding environmental or social activists, the company has to be able to prove that its performance in these areas is really what it says it is. That means that the more objective and verifiable the results, the more meaningful they will be to potential stakeholders. To get to that level, it is possible to use any of three sets of evolving tools.

Tools and Approaches

As was the case in the early days of quality standards, over the past 3 years, there has been a plethora of collaborative approaches, standards, reporting guidelines, compacts, and working groups in this area. This has meant that companies have had to struggle with a sometimes confusing array of offerings; in 2001, an Organization for Economic Cooperation and Development (OECD) study identified 182 initiatives broadly concerned with better corporate behavior. For that reason, it can help simplify the situation by dividing these various tools into three broad categories.

The first set of "tools" among the many initiatives and standards that are emerging falls under the often-used phrase of "aspirational." These include a variety of organizations, initiatives, pledges, and high-level agreements to which companies, NGOs, and sometimes even nations will ascribe. These initiatives vary widely but are usually some form of a macro-level value statement and code of conduct, to be adopted by like-minded companies. More externally focused than the company's own value statement or code of ethical conduct (although they may in fact be used to augment these), they focus on high-level principles concerning employment and the environment to which companies pledge to adhere.

These aspirational standards or initiatives require companies to sign up to endorse these goals of good behavior, in areas such as corporate integrity, labor standards, or environmental policy, but usually don't provide any real direction on what a company needs to do in order to achieve those goals. Seldom requiring any verification or specific measurement or reporting, these types of initiatives and compacts are most valuable for inspiring companies to collaborate and to take these issues seriously. In the end, though, because they have no real enforcement mechanisms, and many critics would contend, no teeth, they leave open the possibility of being used by companies as part of a "greenwash" public relations campaign.

A variation of these tools come with some of the new collaborative initiatives such as the Ethical Trading Initiative (ETI) that are usually made up of a combination of governments, corporations, trade unions, and NGOs. These initiatives may or may not have codes of conduct themselves but cover most of the broad areas such as environment and labor relations that concern socially responsible companies these days. They act as coordinating bodies for promoting general acceptance of other well-recognized codes of conduct.

The second set of tools available to companies are those for reporting on their nonfinancial performance. These tools help companies to publish and boast of their progress against performance goals in areas such as corporate governance, sustainability, employment standards, or environmental policies. These tools are not standards themselves; they don't tell a company how it should behave or what levels of performance would amount to good behavior. Reporting tools are more like accounting standards, describing how to report on the treatment of assets and liabilities in the financial world. And like accounting rules, companies don't actually need to join them in the sense of a club or a compact. They simply need to apply the principles themselves.

The third category of tools, process and performance standards and methodologies, sets out detailed criteria on how a company should meet nonfinancial performance goals. Usually requiring some level of certification, and often independent validation, these standards provide both performance and process-related guidance about how a company should behave and prove that they are behaving with regard to social, environmental, and management policies.

Let's look at the history and composition of each group.

Aspirational Tools

A number of respected groups falling into this category provide both a uniform set of principles and a forum for like-minded organizations to gather and promote important policies such as human rights and environmental sustainability. Two good examples of these are the Global Compact and the Global Sullivan Principles.

The Global Compact

Proposed by United Nations (UN) Secretary General Kofi Annan, the Global Compact was launched in April 2000 as an initiative to bring together UN agencies and the business world in an effort to improve environmental and employment standards in developing countries. Based on nine principles governing behavior in the areas of human rights, labor, and the environment, the compact provides a forum in which companies, NGOs, and government representatives can gather to discuss issues and develop joint projects. These principles state that businesses should:

- Support and respect the protection of internationally proclaimed human rights
- Make sure they are not complicit in human rights abuses
- Uphold the freedom of association and the effective recognition of the right to collective bargaining
- Eliminate all forms of forced and compulsory labor
- Abolish child labour
- Eliminate discrimination in respect of employment and occupation
- Support a precautionary approach to environmental challenges
- Undertake initiatives to promote greater environmental responsibility
- Encourage the development and diffusion of environmentally friendly technologies[3]

The Global Sullivan Principles

The Global Sullivan Principles were originally developed by Reverend Leon H. Sullivan in 1977 as a voluntary code of conduct for companies that were doing business in apartheid South Africa. In 1999, those principles were reissued and made more universally applicable. Similar to the Global Compact in their tone and focus, they invite companies to work toward common goals of human rights, social justice, and economic opportunity. These include support for universal human rights, promoting equal opportunity employment, respecting employees' freedom of association, providing a safe and healthy workplace, and working with governments and communities in which a corporation does business to improve the quality of life for those in the community. Though voluntary, they now request that endorsing companies provide a yearly report on their performance in these areas.[4]

There are potential drawbacks to signing up to these types of compacts, of course, if the company is not really preparing to progress into stage three type of reporting and levels of transparency. "A huge number of corporations are signing these guidelines and compacts," explains Jim Kartalia. "But once a company becomes a signatory their reputation risk has jumped through the roof, because as signatories they are saying they want to be a good corporate citizen. If they don't then have the systems to help them know where they are succeeding or failing, they risk looking hypocritical and the media is going to tear them apart."[5]

Standards of Conduct and Performance Assessment Tools

The second category of tools, standards and codes of conduct, began to emerge in the late 1990s in response to growing indignation by pressure groups, investors, and the public at large, of several decades of corporate violations, both domestically and abroad, concerning employment, health, safety, and the environment. This type of standardization of policies and performance was particularly seen as necessary because of widespread questionable behavior by companies beginning to relocate their manufacturing base in developing world labor markets where there was little government oversight.

Originally begun in desperation by corporations themselves, trying to regulate their environment in developing labor markets, it quickly became obvious that codes of conduct written by individual companies would vary widely and would usually be designed only to portray the company itself in the best possible light. Company codes tended too often to focus only on the easily achievable aspects of labor or environmental policy that went down well with their customers or pressure groups while in fact doing little to improve working conditions or environmental policies in developing markets. In short, self-initiated and self-administered standards did not seem to be working, because they did not generate the trust or reassurance that companies were hoping for.

As with an internal corporate code of conduct, there are several important benefits from applying recognized standards. The first is that it provides some already well-thought-out guidance on the many issues that a company needs to monitor in areas in which catastrophic incidents traditionally occur, such as environmental and product safety policies.

The second reason to adopt standards is that, as with quality initiatives such as Baldrige or ISO 9000, they provide a verifiable indicator of a company's performance, compared with their stated values and with their competition. This "comparability" is at the heart of the standards certification process.

Finally, standards provide a valuable technique for monitoring and correcting quality "faults" in your environmental, safety, employment, or governance processes. In that sense, adopting rigorous standards for nonfinancial reporting is not just for the outside world; it can and should be a valuable operational tool.

These standards can include areas as broad as the workplace or environmental policies or can be more focused on areas of concern to specific industry, for example, banana harvesting best practices or preservation of forests. A variety of these assessment standards and tools have emerged in the past few years, and more are emerging regularly. Some of the most important of these are described in the following sections.

Worker Rights: Social Accountability 8000 and the Ethical Trading Initiative

Among the major efforts occurring today in the area of labor standards, two in particular, stand out: Social Accountability (SA) 8000 and the ETI.

Social Accountability 8000.   One of the most important standards to emerge in the past few years is Social Accountability (SA) 8000, developed by the Council on Economic Priorities Accreditation Agency (CEPAA), a nonprofit organization, first published in 1997. It first emerged as an effort to create a common framework for various companies that had under growing pressure in the early 1990s begun to develop their own codes concerning labor and employment policies, which were inconsistent in their emphasis and impossible to compare or audit. Hoping to create a more consistent set of workplace codes of conduct, Social Accountability International, a standards and advisory group, created the SA 8000 standard, incorporating various best-practice and audit concepts from improvement and quality standards such as ISO 9000 and ISO 14000.

Based on many of the most important ideas taken from the International Labor Organization Conventions, the UN Universal Declaration of Human Rights and the Convention on the Rights of the Child, SA 8000 was one of the first international standards to emerge that was specifically concerned with good labor management and workplace environment practices, particularly in developing-world factories. It was initiated as part of a cooperative effort between various industry groups, labor rights experts and activists, and specialists in certification and auditing and requires employers to provide a safe working environment, to pay sufficient wages, to refuse to employ children or forced or indentured labor, and to limit the work week to no more than 48 hours. It also addresses other key employment issues such as union membership, freedom of association, discrimination, and methods of discipline.

"It [SA 8000] looks at many of the same processes and requirements that government regulations such as OSHA would ask for," says Fitz Hilaire, director of Global Supplier Development at Avon. "It looks at the safety procedures. It looks at the policies that govern your hiring and firing, your methods to ensure there is no discrimination, that there is no child labor and those kinds of things."[6]

BusinessWeek has called SA 8000 "a potential breakthrough not just on sweatshops, but on common labor standards for the global economy as a whole."[7] Under SustainAbility International's guidance,

SA 8000 is both standardized and yet flexible enough to take into account cultural and legal differences of various labor markets. Companies that sign up are provided with a consultancy service, education and training, and a "Guidance Document" that provides them with the codes and guidelines.

And importantly, as part of the SA 8000 standard, companies are required to demonstrate that they are in compliance by submitting to third-party audits that are completed by inspection and audit organizations that have been trained and certified in the SA 8000 methodology.

The Ethical Trading Initiative.   The ETI, on the other hand, is a government-funded project that began in the United Kingdom, and as with so many of today's movements in Europe, it is a collaborative effort between government, businesses, trade unions, and NGOs. Remarkably similar to the SA 8000 in its code of conduct, the ETI strives for a standard application of internationally accepted labor rights codes.

Established in 1998, the ETI involved more than 30 major European companies, 4 trade union groups, and 19 NGOs. The corporate members pledge to observe internationally agreed codes of conduct concerning labor and employment standards that are approved by the ETI and to have their adherence to these standards monitored and audited. Particularly focused on the extended supply chain, member companies must make certain that their suppliers meet agreed standards of conduct within a certain time.

The ETI base code requires that member companies ensure the following:

- Employment is freely chosen.
- Freedom of association and the right to collective bargaining are respected.
- Working conditions are safe and hygienic.
- No child labor is used.

- Workers are paid a living wage.
- Working hours are not excessive.
- No discrimination is practiced.
- Regular employment is provided.
- No harsh or inhumane treatment is allowed.[8]

One obvious problem with a code that contains such elastic clauses as "living wage" or "excessive" hours is that whatever the spirit of the charter, details are left largely undefined, and although it might be nice to assume that any company signing up to the protocol is genuine in its intentions, again, without reporting and verification, skeptics often claim the initiative has no real "teeth."

The ETI, however, is in a sense a testing ground and part of its mandate is to work with suppliers on experimental programs known as "pilot schemes" that develop new methods for improving working conditions based on experimental projects set up with companies, in certain product areas, or in a particular industry or region. Observing the best practices of knowledge management, part of the ETI's mandate is to then distribute these lessons learned both among their corporate membership and broadly throughout the corporate world.

In addition to human rights standards, there are various other topic-specific standards starting to emerge.

Environmental Standards

The 14000 Series   ISO 14000, released initially in 1996 but several times revised, is a global series of environmental management systems (EMSs) standards that provides a framework in which companies can demonstrate their commitment to environmentally responsible policies. As a management standard, it is not based strictly on performance criteria, although it does help companies to establish targets and objectives related to environmental goals. Much like ISO 9000, ISO 14000 serves as a framework that identifies environmental-related processes and activities that companies should be managing.

ISO 14001, the most important of the ISO 14000 standards, focuses on preventing environmental disasters and encourages policies such as full product life-cycle assessment, emissions policies and product labeling. Universally applicable to companies in any industry, it is based on the simple premise that a corporation should think clearly about what it wants to do in the way of environmental management and then to do it in a consistent and reportable way.

Occupational Health and Safety Standards

OHSAS 18000 Series   OHSAS 18001, developed by a group of European standards bodies, is an occupational health and management systems (OHSMS) standard designed to create a safer workplace for employees. It provides guidance to companies for planning and instituting a program of risk management that includes things such as hazard identification, emergency prepardness and response, and the development of policies for recognizing, assessing, and either avoiding or responding to operational hazards, accidents, and incidents.

General Ethical Corporate Behavior for Multinationals Standards

The Organization for Economic Cooperation and Development.   The OECD Guidelines for Multinational Enterprises are a set of voluntary principles and standards that govern many areas of general ethical conduct for businesses. The guidelines cover high-level principles concerning how companies need to interact with other elements of society (such as unions or the local community), as well as providing standards for good business practices involving employment, the environment, bribery, consumers, competition, and taxation.

Risk Management Standards

Standards Australia has developed a risk management standard known as AS/NZS 4360, which provides a framework for an organization's approach to risk management. It is growing in popularity and has already been adopted by companies such as Qantas, Telstra, Pioneer International, and the National Health Service in Britain.

Methodologies for Implementing Standard Codes of Conduct

All of these guidelines are designed to create a high standard of behavior for organizations increasingly doing business in a global environment that is less well controlled by any single government.

AccountAbility (AA) 1000, launched in late 1999 by the Institute of Social and Ethical AccountAbility, on the other hand, is not a standard itself but instead is a key knowledge management methodology for applying those standards. It sets out guidelines that help companies ensure that their reporting process itself is reliable. Although it does have some elements of performance measurement, unlike SA 8000 or the ISO standards, AA 1000 is designed not to direct companies in terms of what the right thing to do is but to instruct them on the way they should go about doing the right thing. It is therefore more a process standard than a performance standard.

AA 1000 has two broad offerings. The first, the AA 1000 Framework, includes a series of modules that provide guidance on how to interact with stakeholders to create the performance indicators, targets, and communications mechanisms consistent with running an ethical company's sustainability policy.

The second offering, the AA 1000S Assurance Standard, provides a method for evaluating performance against specified standards and thus is used usually in combination with a recognized standard such as SA 8000 or ISO 14001. Specifically designed to be consistent with GRI guidelines (see "Reporting Tools," later in this chapter), AA 1000S provides a company with guidance as to the way in which it should apply assurance principles—completeness, materiality, accessibility, evidence—when undertaking the reporting process itself. It therefore helps the company to ensure that readers of its report can be "assured" of its accuracy and authenticity.

It is a framework of tools that allow an organization to do this by covering five areas:

- Planning: Companies work with their stakeholders to create values and objectives and then develop a social and environmental accounting systems, including key performance indicators, measurements, and reporting process.
- Accounting: The company collects and analyzes information on its social and environmental performance and prepares a report.
- Auditing: The performance information and the report are independently audited.
- Reporting: The report is published among employees and stakeholders.
- Embedding: The company takes lessons learned from the process and makes changes to its policies, procedures, and systems in order to improve its performance.[9]

One of the fundamental tenets of AA 1000 is that a broad program of stakeholder engagement is key to understanding and improving social and sustainability policies. The various stakeholders that must be included (e.g., customers, business partners, NGOs, and government agencies) are integral to the performance assessment process.

Despite its considerable complexity, critics of AA 1000 say that the framework is actually better at telling companies what they need to do and is less helpful at explaining how to do it. In many ways, that "how to" advice can best be found (as the authors would probably agree) in other standards such as ISO 14001, using the AA 1000 framework to expand the "stakeholder" consultation side. Still high level and principles based in many key areas, AA 1000 is in the process of being streamlined and improved, and is still very much a work in progress.

Among those improvements, AA 1000 has recently developed five specialized modules, which include the following:

- Assurance framework: A generally accepted accounting practices (GAAP)–like set of accounting principles, process standards, and procedures for social and sustainability auditing, important for creating "comparability" between different company reports.
- Governance and risk management: Designed to help companies to develop performance metrics and to report to investors on the company's efforts to manage social and environmental risk. This module covers issues such as forms of governance, the composition of various governance brokers within a company, how stakeholders gain access to company leaders, how company leaders are involved with ethical and social performance management, incentive programs for promoting sound and ethical performance among employees, and how ethical and social performance is incorporated in decision making.
- Integration of AA 1000 processes with existing management and metrics systems: A module that helps match up information gathering and reporting techniques with standard quality and performance tools such as the balanced scorecard. It provides tools for identifying current systems that can provide governance, social, and environmental reporting information, with guidance on how to prioritize, embed, and integrate the information. This is an important addition, because it helps to link to other well-respected standards.
- Stakeholder engagement: This module provides guidance on how to develop a stakeholder program, including guidelines for addressing conflict of interest issues, tools for assessing the effectiveness of stakeholder engagement programs, and guidelines for documenting the outcomes.
- Accountability in small and medium organizations: This module modifies other elements of the framework in order to help smaller companies participate.[10]

One of the often unappreciated benefits of an approach such as AA 1000 is simply that because stakeholder engagement is so central to the process, the added dialogue and contact with various business partners, activists, and community leaders invariably improves relations and broadens the sources that a company has for early identification of risks. This is especially true if the opinions and concerns of stakeholders are absorbed in a coherent way in a formal management process. Even within the company itself, tools such as surveys and brainstorming help foster better communication and capture employee concerns on an ongoing basis, giving management a better idea of how policies are perceived, followed, or even misunderstood or ignored.

As we will see later, this type of standardized guidance, when combined with performance standards such as SA 8000 or ISO 14001 can help provide companies with a model for implementing the type of integrated ethical framework and risk management process that we are describing in this book, and that are characteristic of progressive stage three and stage four companies. Along with the assurance framework itself, two modules, governance and risk management and integration, are particularly powerful, because they help companies integrate leading governance, risk management, and social and environmental policies into day-to-day business processes. We will look at this more closely in the following sections.

Augmenting Ongoing Quality Standards

As we have seen, although most corporations these days may have several programs in place that promote codes of conduct or accepted standards, whether as part of Equal Opportunities Employer legislation, OSHA, or EPA compliance, these efforts tend to be compartmentalized within organizations, in terms of processes, people, and systems. Broader quality standards such as ISO 9000, Six Sigma, or Baldrige tend to be applied corporation wide, but they tend to be used only to monitor and improve operational performance.

Therefore, even in more progressive organizations, it is not uncommon to have a process for safety, a code of ethics, environmental policy, and a quality movement, with each area managed entirely separately. Too often, the information that these separate processes collect is also held separately.

And it is not just ethical, health and safety, employment, and environmental standards that need to be tied into an integrated ethics and risk management framework. Understanding how well employees are selecting and using pesticides, for example, provides valuable information a variety of issues from employee health and safety to environmental on policies and product safety. It makes sense to capture that knowledge for reporting, for risk management, and for process improvement all at the same time.

REPORTING TOOLS

How do you monitor compliance to these standards among factories in the developing world based just on a code of conduct? The answer, of course, is that you need to audit and report on performance. And obviously, the more objective and verifiable the results the more meaningful they will be to potential stakeholders. This will normally require good knowledge management. In fact, as companies have rushed to produce their own independent social and environmental reports in the past two years, one of the biggest concerns is not underreporting, but overreporting.

As SustainAbility authors note, "Corporate sustainability reporting is in danger of hitting a quality plateau." The average sustainability report, for example, has jumped from 59 pages to 86 pages in the past 2 years (which may not seem much unless you try to read them). SustainAbility calls this "carpet bombing" because readers are bombarded with huge amounts of information, much of which is of questionable relevance.[11]

The carpet-bombing issue, general criticism about the quality and veracity of most company nonfinancial sustainability reports, and the rapidity with which so many independent reporting initiatives are developing combine to make a single consistent reporting method seem attractive. That is one of the reasons why the Global Reporting Initiative has become so relevant in the past 2 years.

The GRI was initiated in 1997 by a U.S.-based group known as the Coalition for Environmentally Responsible Economies (CERES) and is probably the leading reporting initiative today. Working in partnership with the UN Environment Program and a broad group that includes corporations, universities, NGOs, major consultancy and accountancy firms, GRI's mission is to create universally applicable guidelines for social and environmental reporting. This means making sustainability reporting, according to Allen White, the GRI's CEO, "as routine as financial reporting."[12]

To do this, the GRI guidelines provide a framework that explains the principles and procedures that companies need to adopt to prepare a balanced and easily comparable report on environmental, social, and economic performance.

Unlike a code of conduct or a performance standard, the GRI framework doesn't tell a company how it should behave. Based on 57 core and 53 elective performance indicators, the GRI guidelines help to collate the type of wide-ranging information—on emissions, child labor, or data privacy—that is becoming part of standards such as SA 8000 or ISO 14001. Aware that one size does not necessarily fit all, the GRI guidelines now include sector-specific reporting requirements—for tour operators, mining operations, financial services companies, or the automobile industry—to address industry-specific issues.

Critics charge that as with independent reports that carpet bomb the reader, with more than 100 performance indicators, the GRI is itself an invitation to dump huge amounts of information into a company report.

"The depth of the questions is overwhelming at times," charged a Nike representative. "However, the flexibility allowed by the structure makes the GRI more digestible and tenable than most surveys. It can also serve as a useful catalyst in engaging internal leaders in substantive discussion around governance and triple bottom line accountabilities."[13]

Aware of these criticisms, the GRI authors are trying to streamline the process, in part by offering more industry-specific guidelines.

Whatever its faults, the GRI was one of the first recipients of Ted Turner's largesse, receiving a grant for $3 million to help in its development, and the European Commission has essentially endorsed the GRI as the framework upon which to build its own reporting requirements. As of 2003 the GRI had more than 140 major corporations applying its reporting guidelines, including well-known names such as Proctor & Gamble, BASF, Volvo, Electrolux, and Johnson & Johnson.

Issues of Auditing and Verification

Although no company would imagine that it would be trusted to perform its own financial audits or quality certification, many companies are still determined to provide verification of compliance to these internationally recognized standards for social and environmental performance themselves.

Few shareholders and certainly no pressure group is willing to accept a company at its word, issuing a statement of commitment to worthy principles without providing some sort of verifiable evidence of real performance. Obviously, companies will have an incentive to write social and environmental reports that "cherry pick" the areas in which they excel and ignore the areas in which they perform badly. Even if they don't do this, people will suspect that they may have, which means that some form of external verification is necessary in order to bring any credibility to the social and environmental reporting movement.

There are several key characteristics of a good reporting guideline. One of the most important characteristics is that a report must be complete. Corporations have to realize that selectively omitting areas in which they have underperformed is self-defeating.

Keeping in mind the "carpet-bombing" accusations, a report must also be relevant and clear, not overwhelming the reader with irrelevant material that distracts from a good assessment of the company's behavior. Too many reports today are too large, include too much, and defeat even the most determined reader.

Finally, a good report also needs to be accurate and transparent, demonstrating both the bad and the good performance of the company. In addition to mainstream performance data, the best reporters of year 2000 also included information on their prosecutions and fines, environmental liabilities, underachieved targets, and poor performance figures (whether social, environmental, ethical, or economic).

In the end, this conflict over accuracy and transparency, I suspect, and not the difficulty of the process or the lack of a single common standard or approach to reporting, is the real reason most corporations, particularly U.S. corporations, have resisted adopting standardized reporting guidelines. In the litigious U.S. society, many companies are still quite naturally concerned about revealing bad practices.

In fact, the evidence seems to indicate that on the contrary (unless the company is guilty of an egregious violation that it is purposely hiding), reports that lately have emphasized both failures and success weighed against the standards have brought greater kudos for openness than condemnation for any shortcomings. This is particularly true if the company then pledges to work toward improvement.

The failure to use independent third-party auditors for these types of reports, though, is something that continues to undermine the legitimacy of many companies' claims. Third-party scrutiny is considered the "leading practice," and independent verification is already done by most of the top 50 companies that appear on SustainAbility's "Global Reporters 2002 Survey" (Figure 11.2). Some 68 percent of the reports benchmarked in 2003 by SustainAbility had been independently verified. That total was up from 50 percent in 2000 and a frail 28 percent in 1997.[14]

1	The Co-operative Bank
2	Novo Nordisk
3	BAA
4	BT
5	Rio Tinto
6	Royal Dutch/Shell
7	BP
8	Bristol-Meyers Squibb
9	ITT Flygt
10	South African Breweries
11	BASF
12	Volkswagen
13	WIMC
14	CIS Co-operative Insurance
15	Baxter International
16	Cable and Wireless
17	Ricoh Japan
18	Kirin Brewery
19	Chiquita Brands International
20	United Utilities
21	Suncor Energy
22	BC Hydro
23	Eskom
24	Matsushita Electric
25	Manaaki Whenua
26	British Airways
27	SAS
28	Alcan
29	General Motors
30	Henkel
31	Kesko
32	Novartis International
33	Unilever
34	RWE
35	Bayer
36	Deutsche Telekom
37	Procter & Gamble
38	Swiss Re
39	Toyota
40	BMW
41	Tesco
42	AWG
43	Danone
44	AWG
45	Aracruz Celulose
46	Sony
47	Tepco
48	Suez
49	Credit-Suisse
50	Adidas-Salomon

FIGURE 11.2   *SustainAbility's Top 50 Companies, 2002*

Consultants

This need for independent verification not only of the results but also of the process that produced the results has created a need for well-trained, independent third-party auditors. It is a potentially lucrative and growing market, and for the past 2 years in particular, there has been an attempt by many groups to expand into this area. And obviously, as third-party verification becomes the rule, the reputation of the auditor becomes important.

There are three types of independent auditors available for third-party verification of nonfinancial reporting: the traditional large accountancy firm consultants, smaller specialized auditing consultants, and corporate social responsibility (CSR) campaign–related consultancies.

As might be expected, the large, traditional account consultancies such as PriceWaterhouseCoopers, KPMG, and Ernst & Young complete the vast majority of audits. In fact, according to a recent survey, 65 percent of reports reviewed were audited by the major accounting firms.[15] KPMG has its well-established Sustainability Advisory Services that has been operating since the late 1990s. Price-WaterhouseCoopers has a similar Reputational Assurance offering. These companies operate worldwide, of course, which is certainly helpful for audited firms with international operations.

In the U.S., San Francisco-based Business for Social Responsibility is a think tank, conference organizer, and consultancy that has more than 1400 member companies as part of their business forum. It advises on many aspects of standards, reporting, and corporate responsibility generally.

There are also a growing number of smaller, specialized audit consultants that provide assurance for social and environmental reporting in particular. These groups can provide independent assurance services, environmental and social report development, and advice on how to create a sustainability strategy, establish measurable performance goals, and analyze a company's governance policies. They can also help with compliance reviews, benchmarking, and advice on better integration of governance, environmental, social, and economic-monitoring processes.

Coordinating Multiple Audit Efforts

As we have seen, because the base code of many new international standards has been taken from leading practices that are found in quality and productivity standards, there are also many similarities between them. For example, SA 8000 or ISO 14000 have many of the same attributes as Total Quality Management (TQM), Baldridge, or Six Sigma. They are all standards based, all focus on identifying and eliminating "defects" in a process, all are dependent upon some type of quantitative performance measurements, and all require some type of auditing and reporting. There is nothing fundamentally different between social, quality, or environmental reporting. In fact, AA 1000 is essentially an effort to combine the best of the quality movement and apply it to social and environmental reporting.

There is no doubt that there is an affinity between quality, knowledge management, and risk prevention. In fact, the quality and process improvement approaches of the last two decades all have a similar premise. They all attempt to reduce inefficiencies in business processes by continuously identifying and removing "defects" in the way we work. But in doing that, they also use many of the same techniques that are now being adopted for an integrated KRM framework.

For example, each of these quality and improvement regimes relies on some type of quantitative objective analysis. They each have strong, usually team-based programs, that solicit input directly from employees at all levels in the company. They each recognize the importance of involving key leaders, of open reporting, and of closely monitoring environmental health and safety issues. In fact, the Baldridge system already includes many of the aspects of ethical leadership, good governance, and environmental scanning, albeit in a muted form, that that can now be expanded to help an organization actively avoid ethical and legal blunders.

In fact, as Jim Kartalia points out, risk management really begins with implementing a policy for zero tolerance of defects. "If executives can identify a problem, they can prevent it; and the least expensive crisis is the one that is addressed beforehand." This awareness is very important, he says, suggesting that most crises happen without board members being aware of the specific dangers before catastrophe strikes."[16]

Which brings us to a final issue concerning these standards before we move on. It is important to realize that much of what is contained in these standards is not in fact new to most well-functioning and honest companies; they are simply good management practice. It is not uncommon, for that reason, to find that many large and progressive corporations have already put into place over the past several years social, quality, safety, and environmental programs that very much reflect both the spirit and the letter of these standards. For that reason, many companies have begun to coordinate these different often compartmentalized efforts, and this is the important point, through the unifying effect of the actual reporting process itself.

There are many examples of this move by stage three companies to consolidate and coordinate their nonfinancial reporting efforts with ongoing environmental, health, and safety (EHS) initiatives or with quality and productivity improvement certification processes currently in place.

British Telecom, for example, with 28 million fixed phone lines and more than 7.5 million mobile phone customers, has a broad set of environmental programs already in place concerning waste, fuel, and emissions and energy usage. It has implemented ISO 14001 to cover all of its operations in the United Kingdom as part of an environmental management system, in part as an attempt to achieve broad efficiency savings and in part to coordinate the many different environmentally related projects going on in the company. Its recycling program, in effect for several years, now recycles nearly one third of the company's total waste while at the same time reducing waste to landfill by 5.6 percent. This focus on waste recycling saves them more than $4 million each year on landfill tax alone. At the same time, the company has focused on improving its fleet size and efficiency and in the last decade has reduced company energy usage by 23 percent, saving more than $6 million during the same period.

Chris Tuppen, head of Sustainable Development and Corporate Accountability at British Telecom, says that ISO 14001 helps bring a "more systematic approach" to the process and an overall coordination to these many projects, helping British Telecom to more tightly define roles and responsibilities, initiating wider involvement among operational divisions, and helping it to more accurately measure its savings.[17]

Similarly, Intel had various long-standing EHS programs that had already been completing some form of compliance auditing for some time, including some 200 assessments done each year worldwide on its suppliers. The company already maintains control of waste products and ships these back from its various sites in developing countries in order to avoid having to burn the materials. Its Product Ecology group looks at all issues concerning manufacturing, use, and disposal of products, and these efforts are coordinated with its Issues Prevention and Management group, which serves as the company's risk management function, providing both the early alert and incident management activities for the company. That group is also tied directly into Intel's customer service centers, which screen for any social, environmental, or ethical issues and forward those issues to the Issues Prevention group and other appropriate departments. These several departments then meet with the CSR department on a regular basis to coordinate activities company-wide.

In fact, given that the methods for information collection and often the stakeholders themselves are the same, it is not surprising that several progressive companies already combine at least their social, quality, and environmental audits.

"Combined audits save both time and money," contends Deborah Leipziger, European director for Social Accountability International and co-author of *Corporate Citizenship: Successful Strategies of Responsible Companies*. She found that companies like Avon and BVOI were already combining some elements of their audits for quality and social issues. Although quality, social, and environmental auditing can be very different, areas such as record checking, interviews, and management review can be integrated.

"There are inherent synergies between social and environmental auditing. In fact, there is a clear synergy between ISO 14000 (environmental) and SA 8000 in the specific area of health and safety, since auditors look closely at those environmental issues which might impact directly or indirectly on the health and well-being of the workers."[18]

It is also interesting to see that corporate governance is increasingly being included as a part of these reporting efforts. After all, as we have seen, the combination of management structure and style is very much an indicator of company attitudes toward ethics, values, and social and environmental risks. As South African Breweries, a strong advocate of sustainability reporting, says in its latest sustainability report, "It makes sense from a corporate perspective that governance is the lead agent, not only in consolidating aspects of corporate citizenship, CSR and sustainable development, but also in integrating these agendas into mainstream business activities."[19]

This movement to integrate the several reporting processes with existing quality, productivity, and safety processes—processes that might be occurring simultaneously in various functional silos in the company—is a defining characteristic of a progressive stage three company. In many ways, they are making an important step toward "Total Quality and Risk Management."

There are many advantages to this approach. It is more cost effective, of course, in that the same team needs to interview employees or other stakeholders only once. A single interview and inspection team also reduces disruption on the factory floor, and other tools such as surveys can be combined for time and cost savings. Although quality audits are much less dependent on these types of employee interviews, and the three streams are not always compatible, synergies are certainly driving companies to combine these teams as much as possible.

One problem with social and economic reporting, however, is that although many of the information collection methods—surveys, interviews, inspections—are the same between, say, an EHS audit and an ISO 14001 survey, there tends to be a different vocabulary used when actually producing the reports themselves. Part of the reason for this is simply that different audiences require different terminology and nomenclature. What is appropriate for environmental pressure groups or regulators may not always be meaningful to analysts, investors, and financial markets. After all, these have traditionally been two very different audiences. For this reason, GRI and several other reporting standards are assiduously trying to find a common vocabulary, as well as legitimate links, between the three legs of the triple–bottom-line accounting process, something that will be more helpful to financial markets in particular.

Socially Responsible Investing

One final area that should be discussed with regard to promoting ethical behavior in companies is socially responsibility investing (SRI).

SRI (i.e., investing only in companies that demonstrate that they adhere to high governance, social, and environmental standards) continues to provide another strong reason why companies should actively manage risks in these areas and begin to produce reliable reports that reflect their good behavior. In fact, despite early fears by analysts that limiting investment opportunities to only "ethical" companies would never be an acceptable risk to investors (in that a focus on "ethical" companies alone would create unacceptable exposure because of a lack of diversification), SRI has actually become quite a legitimate feature of investing today. According to a survey by Harris Interactive, 71 percent of Americans say they consider corporate citizenship when they make investment decisions.[20]

And maybe surprisingly, there is mounting evidence that SRI funds tend to do well, sometimes outperforming the market average. The Dow Jones Sustainability Group Index (DJSGI) looked at 200 companies in its index from various industry sectors and concluded that they "significantly outperformed" the overall Dow Jones index between 1995 and 2000. A survey by McKinsey found that "high standards of corporate governance" can result in a share price premium of up to 20 percent.[21]

According to Ethical Performance, there are now more than 60 ethical trusts in the United Kingdom, and according to A.D. Little, assets in professionally managed, socially screened investment portfolios rose by 36 percent between 1999 and 2001. The total level of socially and environmentally responsible investing in the United States rose 8 percent from $2.16 trillion to $2.34 trillion in that same period. This means that about one of every eight dollars under professional management in the United States is invested in companies that have been screened for key ethical attributes.[22] Calvert, the U.S. consultancy and mutual fund managers, announced a similar finding, when it estimated in a recent study that within the next decade, SRI will represent up to 10 percent of all U.S. mutual fund assets.

Canada has its Jantsi Social Investment Index (JSI), and both the U.S. Down Jones' Sustainable Asset Management and the British FTSE4 Good indices screen for company performance in nonfinancial areas such as strategic planning, corporate governance, environmental reporting, corruption policies, human rights issues, and environmental product design and disposal policies. FTSE4 Good, the ethical indices for the FTSE in London, screens companies on these issues, adding categories of "impact" risk, with those in high-risk industries such as energy, petroleum, or water expected to produce publicly available reports on their approach to social and environmental management.

In fact, there was a time not so long ago that the business press was predicting that this type of ethics- and risk-screening process would revolutionize the way companies behaved and the way that they reported on their behavior. After all, institutional pension fund holders, such as the state of California or the AFL/CIO, have pledged to shift billions of dollars worth of their enormous portfolios to only

those indices that screened for good environmental and social policies. The California Public Employees Retirement System, for
example, is the United States's largest pension fund (more than $150
billion in managed assets) and is one of the leading proponents of
activism in this area.[23] With this sort of money at stake, they have
enormous leverage to influence company behavior.

Of course, fund managers themselves have taken responsibility for
much of this screening. Calvert fund management offers 18 socially
screened funds and completes research on 1000 domestic and international companies each year, looking at various nonfinancial performance criteria in areas such as management accountability, incentive
structures, ethical enforcement programs, and the adoption of standards and guidelines for social and environmental performance. These
are the sort of criteria that are more often being used to assess
company stability, particularly as the legitimacy and value of financial
reports have been so badly undermined with recent scandals.[24] Even
many asset managers who do not deal specifically in SRI funds now
examine both the balance sheet and the proxy statements when selecting stocks. They too recognize that financial numbers alone can
mislead and that equally important to scrutinize a corporation's management, risk, and corporate governance policies.

A number of groups specialize in providing investors with independent research on a company's corporate governance or social and
environmental policies. Every major industrial nation now has many
of these groups, organizations such as the IRRC (Investors Responsibility Research Center) in Britain or the Center for Responsible
Business (CRB) in the United States, EthicScan in Canada, the
Japanese Research Institute in Japan, the Center for Australian Ethical
Research (CAER) in Australia, and many more in Europe, including
EIRIS, which researches more than 2500 companies from around the
world. These groups supply investors with key information on a
company's ethical and risk polices, adding another layer to the growing
number of analysts and interest groups that continue to put increased
scrutiny on companies worldwide.

Similarly, in the United Kingdom, the association of British Insurers—representing corporations that control 20 percent of the United Kingdom stock market—has now published guidelines for companies that include a requirement for reporting on their policies for managing risks in social and environmental policy. In fact, U.K. law also now requires pension fund trustees to declare how they use social, environmental, and ethical issues when making their investment decisions. Australia passed a similar requirement under its Financial Services Reform Act that took effect in March 2003, whereby all investment firms are required to disclose "the extent to which labor standards or environmental, social, or ethical considerations are taken into account."[25]

Many critics rightly contend that the standards for inclusion in these ethical indices tend to be very low; and there has been a good deal of criticism about Dow's SAM indices selecting companies such as British American Tobacco, a company that has applied AA 1000 standards and has won awards for its social and environmental reporting (proving that a company can produce what could be deemed a socially irresponsible product in a socially responsible way).

Others, like Hewitt Roberts of Entropy International are more sanguine about the role of SRI. "At the end of the day CSR and good corporate governance will become the normal way of doing business—there will be no funds other than ethical funds—because they are not sustainable in the long run if they do not provide the necessary kind of investment governance and investment guarantees."

"You can see this in the growing participation in CSR and corporate governance communities, whether they be forums, conferences or trade shows, online Web arenas, membership groups like AccountAbility, or social investment forums themselves."

"The importance, participation, and involvement in these areas has skyrocketed," Roberts concludes, "growing enormously in the blink of an eye. This is very different from the environmental movement that started with the 'Silent Spring' a decade or two or three before it became a major mass movement. CSR is occurring much quicker than

was the case for the environmental performance improvement movement, and with much greater magnitude and reach."[26]

Whether SRI standards ever become the driving force behind corporate reporting may not matter in the end. Whatever its limitations,
SRI is still another significant pressure on companies to move toward
nonfinancial reporting and to demonstrate that they have a cogent risk
management policy in place.

The Value of Standards

There are many benefits to adopting these types of standards-based
programs. First, it helps you to put your ethical code of conduct into
practice at an operational level, ensuring that corporate governance,
environmental, and social behavior are all aligned with your values and
ethical principles. And, of course, a company gets possibly the greatest benefit of all simply from the discipline of completing the process
of ethical, social, and environmental auditing, in that any systematic
review and reporting on performance will reveal organizational policy
weaknesses and dangerous practices, simply because they are reviewed
regularly and placed in an ethical and risk management context.

Second, the very exercise of recognizing, implementing, and monitoring adherence to these standards can help a company realize significant improvements, in efficiency savings, in recycling, in reduced
employment turnover, and in higher rates of labor productivity.
When combined with quality standards, the initiative can be a much
more comprehensive way of monitoring and employing quality and
improvement techniques. Even as stand-alone, for many companies
this type of reporting exercise would be helpful, because it combines
good behavior with good business.

Third, adopting internationally recognized standards provides a
company with valuable monitoring and audit information to detect
health, safety, or labor activities that could potentially put the company
at risk. It, in effect, becomes the second key structure of a company's
integrity and risk framework.

Finally, standards, particularly when independently verified, help a company differentiate itself from its competition and become a candidate for "ethical" investors.

CHAPTER ENDNOTES

[1] "Beyond Numbers," *KPMG Assurance and Advisory Services Booklet*, 2002, p. 1.

[2] "Beyond Numbers," *KPMG Assurance and Advisory Services Booklet*, 2002, p. 17.

[3] "The Global Compact: Corporate Leadership in the World Economy," *Global Compact Office*, The United Nations, January 2001.

[4] The Global Sullivan Principles Web site. Available at globalsullivanprinciples.org.

[5] Jim Kartalia, interviewed by the author, January 23, 2003.

[6] Davil Creelman, "Interview: Avon's Fitz Hilaire on Social Accountability," *Star Tribune*. Available from startribune.hr.com/hrcom/index.cfm/weeklymag/F754EEA5-73D8-4CB9-98D56A615F9EBB72?ost=wmfeature.

[7] Social Accountability International's Web site. Available from www.cepaa.org/introduction.htm.

[8] The Ethical Trade Initiative Web site. Available from www.ethicaltrade.org/pub/publications/purprinc/en/index.shtml.

[9] "AA 1000 Assurance Standard: Guiding Principles," Consultation Document, *AccountAbility*, June 2002.

[10] "AA 1000 Assurance Standard: Guiding Principles," Consultation Brief, *AccountAbility*, March 2002.

[11] Alison Maitland, "Truants, Nerds and Supersonics," *Financial Times*, November 18, 2002.

[12] Tim Dickson, "The Financial Case for Behaving Responsibly," *Financial Times*, August 19, 2002.

[13] Mallen Baker, "The Global Reporting Initiative—raising the bar too high?" *Ethical Corporation Magazine*, October 2002, p. 39.

[14] "Beyond Numbers," *KPMG Assurance and Advisory Services Booklet*, 2002, p. 17.

[15] "Beyond Numbers," *KPMG Assurance and Advisory Services Booklet*, 2002, p. 17.

[16] Jim Kartalia, "Reputation at Risk?" *Risk Management*, May 2000. Available from www.rims.org/mmag.

[17] Conference discussion with Chris Tuppen, November 2002; and "Case Studies, BT: Staying online with ISO 14001," 2001 Business in the Environment, Ernst & Young.

[18] Deborah Leipziger, "Integrating Audits: The Holy Grail of the Auditing World," *Business Minds.com*. Available from www.business-minds.com/article.asp?item=48.

[19] Alison Maitland, "Truants, Nerds and Supersonics," *Financial Times*, November 18, 2002, p. 9.

[20] "Consumers Skeptical of Corporate Citizenship Activities," *Holmes Report*, April 25, 2002, p. 1. Available from www.holmesreport.com.

[21] Rikki Stancich, "Analysis Whether Desperate Times Demand Desperate Measures," *Ethical Corporation*, August 22, 2002. Available from www.ethicalcorp.com/newstemplate.asp?idnum=332.

[22] "2001 Report on Socially Responsible Investing Trends in the United States," *SIF Industry Research Program*, 18 November 2001. Available from www.socialinvest.org.

[23] AlisonMaitland, "Scandals Draw Attention to 'Superficial' Measures," *Financial Times*, 10 December 2002, p. IV.

[24] Calvert, "Calvert Social Responsibility Criteria," *Calvert Asset Management*, 2002.

[25] William Baue, "Australia To Require Investment Firms to Disclose How They Take SRI into Account," *Social Funds.com*, 3 January 2003. Available from www.socialfunds.com/news/print.cgi?sfarticleid=998.

[26] Hewitt Roberts, interviewed by the author, February 13, 2003.

About the Author

Dale Neef is an author and strategic management consultant, specializing in company supply chain and risk management issues. A veteran of many enterprise-wide procurements, Enterprise Resource Planning, and change management projects, he has worked for IBM and CSC and was a fellow at Ernst & Young's Center for Business Innovation. He has a doctorate from Cambridge University, was a research fellow at Harvard, and apart from TV and radio commentary and frequent contributions to journals, has written or edited numerous books on business and the economy, including *e-Procurement: From Strategy to Implementation*, *The Knowledge Economy*, *The Economic Impact of Knowledge*, and *A Little Knowledge is a Dangerous Thing*.

Index